THE LIE

And Other
BIBLICAL TRUTHS
about the **COMING TRIBULATION**

Greg Harris

© 2021 Gregory H. Harris
The Lie—
And Other Biblical Truths about the Coming Tribulation

All rights reserved. No part of this book may be reproduced or transmitted in any form or by any means, electronic or mechanical, including photocopying, recording, or by any information storage and retrieval system, without permission in writing from the publisher.

Glory Books Ministry
www.glorybooks.org
ISBN: **9781737243543**
Scripture taken from the NEW AMERICAN STANDARD BIBLE®,
Copyright © 1960,1962,1963,1968,1971,1972,1973,1975,1977
by The Lockman Foundation. Used by permission.

Full Bibliographic Info

Chapter One—Gregory H. Harris, "Satan's Work as a Deceiver," *Bibliotheca Sacra*. 156:2 (Apr–June 1999), 190–202. Used by permission.

Chapter Two—Gregory H. Harris, "Satan's Deceptive Miracles in the Tribulation," *Bibliotheca Sacra*. 156:3 (July–Sept 1999), 308–24. Used by permission.

Chapter Three— Gregory H. Harris "Does God Deceive? Towards a Biblical Understanding of the 'Deluding Influence' of 2 Thessalonians 2:11," *The Master's Seminary Journal* 16:1 (Spring 2005), 73–93. Used by permission.

Chapter Four—Gregory H. Harris, "The Wound of the Beast in the Tribulation," *Bibliotheca Sacra*. 156:4 (Oct–Dec 1999), 459–68. Used by permission.

Chapter Five—Gregory H. Harris, "Can Satan Raise the Dead? Toward a Biblical View of the Beast's Wound," *The Master's Seminary Journal* 18:1 (Spring 2007), 23–41. Used by permission.

Chapter Six—Gregory H. Harris, "Premillennialism in the New Testament: Five Biblically Doctrinal Truths," *The Master's Seminary Journal* 29:2 (Fall 2018), 177–205. Used by permission.

For even though they knew God, they did not honor Him as God or give thanks, but they became futile in their speculations, and their foolish heart was darkened.

Professing to be wise, they became fools, and exchanged the glory of the incorruptible God for an image in the form of corruptible man and of birds and four-footed animals and crawling creatures.

Therefore, God gave them over in the lusts of their hearts to impurity, so that their bodies would be dishonored among them.

For they exchanged the truth of God for a lie [literally, "the lie"] and worshiped and served the creature rather than the Creator, who is blessed forever. Amen.

—Romans 1:21–25

BOOK DEDICATION

Normally we end up dedicating the book to someone or a group of people. As I more and more hand Glory Books over to beloved people, I wanted to **thank you all** who had any part in this—big, small, or just prayed or encouraged one way or another.

I tell people quite often to "Walk with God, and you will not miss His will. You may not understand it for a while, but you will not miss God's Will."

Glory Books is one of those. I bucked, kicked, dragged my fingers on the sidewalk—so to speak—and nevertheless, here we are. I'll wait and let God show you some of the things He did and how He used this association that He had put together.

I think it would surprise you. It certainly surprised me.

God bless you all,

Greg Harris
June 2021

CREDITS

Dr. Greg Harris' personal editor: Patricia Rotisky

Associate editor: Chris Fowler

Dr. Greg Harris' website: www.glorybooks.com

<u>TMS consulting class</u>: "The Master's Seminary consulting class," Spring 2021: Bob and Julie Fanciullacci, Becky Howard, Rob Thurman, Nancy Anderson, Tricia Steiger, Andre Randolph [*Emeritus*], Faly Ravoahangy [*Emeritus*], Premend Choy [*Emeritus*], Dave Owen, Chad Tucker, and Chris Fowler.

—<u>And those untimely born and grafted in:</u> Kevin Laymon, Aaron Filburn, Bill and Lalanne Barber, and Chazz Anderson, King Charles Clemons.

Ongoing thanks to Dr. Bill Barrick for his godly scholarship and Brotherhood.

INTRODUCTION AND BRIEF EXPLANATION

Since my diagnosis of a terminal disease, and major side effects of some very strong medicine that I am on, I have not been racing wildly, but I certainly have tried to redeem the time, purposefully considering the situation. Until recently, things were fine, and it was a very productive segment of time for me. As I was preparing and writing a bit of *The Lie—And Other Biblical Truths About the Coming Tribulation*, godly friends intervened and told me it was time to stop writing; that the standard of writing had dropped considerably.

I had made peace with that and was looking for something to do, because I had spent virtually every day of the past 5 to 6 years, including this Introduction in mid-2021, writing in some way. I was looking for something the Lord would have me do, but I was not sure what to do.

I was informed by a close friend who knew the situation very well, that some of my journal articles, already edited and published, would make up between 85% to 90% of what I had planned to include in *The Lie*. Of course, using different journal articles to cover the material meant that not everything would be in perfect order, and that one journal article might contain four or five different items from the same biblical chapter. I tried to have very little overlap, but some of it could not be helped.

So, under my no-other-option than use the journal articles to produce this book by how I just described, I am only using materials from previously published journal articles, including their footnotes. Special thanks to Dallas Theological Seminary for permission to reprint my journal articles in *Bibliotheca Sacra* (the name of their periodical journal), and thanks to The Master's Seminary for allowing me to use some of the articles I published with their journal, entitled the *Master's Seminary Journal*.

A few final points to note: first, just for clarity's sake, in the Table of Contents we have put in only the chapters' names (which are actually the titles for the individual journal articles). I think you will see how much easier they are to read. Second, the full bibliographic entries will be on the first page and the end of the book. Third, I purposely wrote my journal articles to meet the academic standard, but also—and this is important to know—I wrote them for people in the church to read. So, do not let the concept of journal articles discourage you from reading this book. There may be a few words or contents that need explaining, but I tried to do that whenever I wrote.

If you have not seen the massive differences of interpretation between the premillennial understanding of Scripture versus the amillennial, we will clearly view both positions side by side, with their supporting quotes from some of their stalwarts. We will set forth different approaches to Scripture as we study the Book of Revelation, and these are not some minor issues. So much of how one interprets Scripture ties in with those views.

And who knows, maybe that was one reason God wanted *The Lie* to be written.

TABLE OF CONTENTS

Book Dedication v

Credits vi

Introduction and Brief Explanation vii

Chapter 1: Satan's Work as a Deceiver 1

Chapter 2: Satan's Deceptive Miracles in the Tribulation 16

Chapter 3: Does God Deceive? Towards a Biblical Understanding of the 'Deluding Influence' of 2 Thessalonians 2:11 36

Chapter 4: The Wound of the Beast in the Tribulation 66

Chapter 5: Can Satan Raise the Dead? Toward a Biblical View of the Beast's Wound 78

Chapter 6: Premillennialism in the New Testament: Five Biblically Doctrinal Truths 105

The Lie

TABLE OF CONTENTS

Dedication iv

Credits vi

Introduction and Brief Explanation vii

Chapter 1. Satan's Wiles as a Deceiver 1

Chapter 2. Satan's Deceptive Miracles in the Tribulation 20

Chapter 3. Does God Lie to Us? Toward a Biblical Understanding of the Debated Influences of 2 Thessalonians 2:11 30

Chapter 4. The Wound of the Beast in the Tribulation 60

Chapter 5. Can Satan Raise the Dead? Toward a Biblical View of the Bible's Wording 74

Chapter 6. Pseuditheomania in the New Testament: Five Biblically Accepted Truths 102

CHAPTER 1

SATAN'S WORK AS A DECEIVER

Gregory H. Harris

The Bible presents Satan as playing a strategic role in deceiving people so that they either do not receive or do not retain the truth of God. By deceptive tactics Satan continually attempts to hinder God's program. Deception is an essential element of Satan's nature, for Jesus said he is "a murderer from the beginning, and does not stand in the truth, because there is no truth in him. Whenever he speaks a lie, he speaks from his own nature; for he is a liar, and the father of lies" (John 8:44). Lying is one of his basic means of deceiving others.

The apostle John wrote of "the great dragon . . . the serpent of old who is called the devil and Satan, who deceives the whole world" (Rev. 12:9). The word "deceives" renders a present active participle (ὁ πλανῶν), which speaks of deception that is "a continuous action which has become . . . habitual."[1] Satan is involved in much more than random occurrences; he deceives because it is part of his personality to do so.

Gregory H. Harris is Assistant Professor of Bible Exposition, Southeastern Baptist Theological Seminary, Wake Forest, North Carolina.

[1] Fritz Rienecker, *A Linguistic Key to the Greek New Testament*, ed. Cleon L. Rogers, Jr. (Grand Rapids: Zondervan, 1980), 839.

Two Old Testament accounts depict Satan's use of deception to accomplish his goals.[2] Of utmost importance is the account of the fall of man. Although the word "deception" is not specifically used in Genesis 3, Paul twice identified Satan's role in the Garden of Eden as deception. In 2 Corinthians 11:3 he wrote, "But I am afraid, lest as the serpent deceived Eve by his craftiness, your minds should be led astray from the simplicity and purity of devotion to Christ." And in 1 Timothy 2:14 Paul wrote that "it was not Adam who was deceived, but the woman being quite deceived, fell into transgression." In both verses Paul used an intensified form of the verb "deceive" (ἐξαπατάω, rather than ἀπατάω).[3]

The other significant Old Testament reference depicting Satan as a deceiver is more enigmatic. First Chronicles 21:1 states that "Satan stood up against Israel and moved David to number Israel." Although again the specific word "deception" is not used here, deception is evident in that Satan targeted David to lead him into sin, and David and Israel suffered the consequences of his actions. The parallel account in 2 Samuel 24 shows the seriousness of this transgression and the subsequent punishment inflicted on David and the nation. This account shows Satan may work behind the scenes in ways not discernible by human means. No one would have known of Satan's role in this incident unless God revealed it.

In explaining the parable of the tares sown among the wheat, Jesus said "the enemy who sowed them is the devil" (Matt. 13:39). This account reveals that Satan currently engages in acts of deception that will continue until the end of the age. In addition to this, so adept is Satan's sowing of the false seed among the true that the false seed will be properly identified and separated only at the consummation of the age

---

[2] Hiebert rightly notes that it is remarkable that relatively few references are made in the Old Testament to Satan as the great adversary of God and His people. The full picture of Satan's evil character is developed in the New Testament (D. Edmond Hiebert, "Satan," in *Zondervan Pictorial Encyclopedia of the Bible,* ed. Merrill C. Tenney [Grand Rapids: Zondervan, 1975], 5:282).

[3] Paul employed ἐξαπατάω whenever prevalent, intentional, and massive deception was involved (Ernest Best, *A Commentary on the First and Second Epistles to the Thessalonians,* Black's New Testament Commentaries [London: Adam & Clark, 1972], 280). This intensified form also is found in reference to the deceit of sin (Rom. 7:11) and deception wrought by false teachers (16:18).

(vv. 28-30). Deception obviously continues to be a highly effective weapon for Satan and will remain so until the Lord returns.

Paul wrote that "Satan disguises himself as an angel of light" (2 Cor. 11:14). The apostle then added that Satan's deception is carried out by false apostles who "also disguise themselves as servants of righteousness" (v. 15). In Romans 16:17-20 Paul warned against false teachers in the church who by "their smooth and flattering speech . . . deceive the hearts of the unsuspecting" (v. 18). The ultimate source of their deception is by Satan, for as Paul wrote, "the God of peace will soon crush Satan under your feet" (v. 20). So even human agents who deceive others inside the church can ultimately be associated with the deceptive tactics employed by Satan.

However, Satan also uses demons to deceive the world. First Timothy 4:1-2 warns of "deceitful spirits"[4] who will disseminate their doctrines and deceive many. John noted both the spiritual and human factors involved when he warned, "Beloved, do not believe every spirit, but test the spirits to see whether they are from God; because many false prophets have gone out into the world" (1 John 4:1). Once more the source of such deceivers is indicated in that "every spirit that does not confess Jesus is not from God; and this is the spirit of the antichrist, of which you have heard that it is coming, and now it is already in the world" (v. 3).

Still another example of Satan's current use of deception as one of his primary means of operation is found in 1 Timothy 3:7. In giving guidelines for the qualifications of an elder Paul stated that one who qualifies for this office "must have a good reputation with those outside the church, so that he may not fall into reproach and the snare of the devil." The word "snare" ($παγίς$) was used of traps set for catching wild birds. It later came to be used of anything that brought sudden and unexpected danger or death.[5] The same word is used in 2 Timothy 2:26 in reference to those who may eventually "come to their senses and

---

[4] The phrase $πνεύμασιν πλάνοις$ is literally "deceiving (or seducing) spirits".

[5] George W. Knight III, *Commentary on the Pastoral Epistles*, New International Greek Testament Commentary (Grand Rapids: Eerdmans, 1992), 165-66. This word is also used in Luke 21:34; Romans 11:9; and 1 Timothy 6:9.

escape from the snare of the devil." Obviously a certain amount of deception is needed in order for a snare to work, even if only to catch birds.

However, as ruinous as Satan's previous and present works of deception have been and are, the Bible indicates that a future time of intensified satanic deception will occur during the Tribulation, a time unparalleled in human history. In the Olivet Discourse Jesus repeatedly predicted this future deception. In Matthew 24:4-5 He said, "See to it that no one misleads you. For many will come in My name, saying, 'I am the Christ,' and will mislead many." This future deception will be extensive and highly effective. Jesus added that additional religious elements will be associated with this deception: "Many false prophets will arise, and will mislead many" (v. 11). Miraculous elements will be employed in accomplishing this deception: "For false Christs and false prophets will arise and will show great signs and wonders, so as to mislead, if possible, even the elect. Behold, I have told you in advance" (vv. 24-25; see also Mark 13:22-23). Thus individuals living before or during that time are to be forewarned; they will have no legitimate excuse for allowing themselves to be deceived.

In writing to the Thessalonian believers who were concerned they were living in the Day of the Lord, Paul also referred several times to the deception that will accompany that future period. Having comforted the Thessalonians that they most assuredly were not in the Tribulation (2 Thess. 2:1-2, 5), Paul began his instruction on eschatological events partly by describing the deception associated with that period as well as the need to avoid it. He strongly cautioned the believers, "Let no one in any way deceive you" (v. 3). He forewarned of one who will come as a satanically empowered agent "with all the deception of wickedness for those who perish" (vv. 9-10). In fact, this deception in the Tribulation will be intensified by God Himself. "God will send upon them a deluding influence so that they might believe what is false" (v. 11).[6] Thus a time

---

[6] "What is false" is a rather loose translation. Literally, what many people of that time will believe is "the lie" (τῷ ψεύδει). From this verse alone it is obvious that the deception of that period will not be a collection of random efforts at deception. A particular lie will be substituted for the truth.

of intense deception will occur during the Tribulation, a deception that will be magnified by satanic works, and one that will be centered around "the lie" of the one who will serve as Satan's earthly regent.

Also, the apostle John made significant statements regarding present satanic deception as well as the future deception associated with the Antichrist. Regarding the false teachers of his day who were erroneous in both their teaching and lifestyle, John forewarned the believers by writing, "These things I have written to you concerning those who are trying to deceive you" (1 John 2:26), and "Little children, let no one deceive you" (3:7). John observed, "Many deceivers have gone out into the world, those who do not acknowledge Jesus Christ as coming in the flesh. This is the deceiver and the antichrist" (2 John 2:7). John referred to Satan as the one "who deceives [ἀπατάω] the whole world" (Rev. 12:9) and deceives "the nations" (20:3).

THE MEANING OF DECEPTION

The two words rendered "to deceive" are πλανάω and ἀπατάω. Since the two terms are used interchangeably throughout Scripture, no major distinction seems to exist.[7]

The more common word used for the deception in the Tribulation is πλανάω, "to cause to wander, lead astray,"[8] or "to lead astray, mislead by means of deception."[9] The passive tense can be rendered "to let oneself be misled, deceived."[10]

A derivative of the verb πλανάω frequently used in reference to tribulational deception is the noun πλάνη. It is variously defined as

---

[7] G. B. Winer, *Grammar of the Idiom of the New Testament*, trans. J. Henry Thayer (Andover, MA: Flagg and Gould, 1825, reprint, Andover, MA: Draper, 1970), 500.

[8] George Abbott-Smith, *A Manual Lexicon of the New Testament* (Edinburgh: Clark, 1952), 363.

[9] Henry George Liddell and Robert Scott, A *Greek-English Lexicon*, 9th ed., rev. Henry Stuart Jones (Oxford: Clarendon, 1940), 2:1411.

[10] Walter Bauer, William F. Arndt, and F. Wilbur Gingrich, *A Greek-English Lexicon of the New Testament and Other Early Christian Literature*, 2d ed., rev. F. Wilbur Gingrich and Frederick W. Danker (Chicago: University of Chicago Press, 1979), 665. Compare similar usage in Matthew 24:24, Luke 21:8, John 7:47, and Revelation 18:23.

"wandering, roaming . . . wandering from the path of truth, error, delusion, deceit, deception to which one is subject."[11] In all the passages where πλάνη occurs in the New Testament,[12] it "has the passive meaning of 'error,' though the active meaning of 'deceit' would sometimes be equally appropriate."[13]

Gottleib Lünemann underscores the significance of this type of deception in contrast to the standard of God's truth: "πλάνη denotes a deliberate 'deceitfulness' and always stands in contrast to ἀλήθεια ['truth']. The context determines more precisely what is 'the truth' and in turn what is 'the deceit.' In 1 Thessalonians 2:3 Paul states, 'For our exhortation does not come from error or impurity or by way of deceit....' In this sense Paul insisted that his doctrine was not fiction, a whim, a dream, nor a delusion. It was founded upon the opposite of deceit with the divine truth as his source."[14] Gottleib Lünemann's remarks are especially appropriate in view of the fact that Paul later used πλάνη in 2 Thessalonians 2:11 in reference to the deluding influence God will send, which will become a means of judgment against those who reject Him and His truth (2:12).

Braun states that in the Tribulation ungodly powers will lead the world astray by carrying out massive deception.[15] In other words this future deception cannot transpire until deceptive agents appear. Although Braun refers to these powers as presented in "mythical garb" and "all [are] taken from the world of apocalyptic myth," he nonetheless notes

---

[11] Ibid., 671.

[12] A pertinent observation may be made regarding the use of πλάνος in 2 John 7: "For many deceivers [πλάνοι] have gone out into the world, those who do not acknowledge Jesus Christ as coming in the flesh. This is the deceiver [ὁ πλάνος] and the antichrist." It is ironic that the Pharisees used the same word to refer to Jesus. They called Him "that deceiver [ἐκεῖνος ὁ πλάνος]" (Matt. 27:63). They further reasoned that "the last deception [πλάνη] will be worse than the first" (v. 64).

[13] Joseph Armitage Robinson, *St. Paul's Epistle to the Ephesians*, 2d ed. (London: James Clarke, 1903), 185.

[14] Gottleib Lünemann, "First and Second Thessalonians," in *Meyer's Critical and Exegetical Commentary on the New Testament* (Edinburgh: Clark, 1880), 46.

[15] Herbert Braun, "πλανάω" in *Theological Dictionary of the New Testament*, 6 (1968), 246–49.

that deception then will hinge around these agents, whether suprahuman or mortal, who will be used in bringing about the deception.[16]

Like its synonym πλανάω, ἀπατάω also conveys the idea of deceiving, cheating, or misleading someone.[17] 'Απατάω is not used nearly so much as πλανάω and is found only in later Greek writings.[18] Paul used the verb ἀπατάω only once. In Ephesians 5:6 he warned, "Let no one deceive [ἀπατάτω] you with empty words, for because of these things the wrath of God comes upon the sons of disobedience." Concerning the deception of the Tribulation Paul employed the intensified form ἐξαπατάω.[19] In writing to young believers who erroneously thought they were in the midst of the Day of the Lord, he cautioned, "Let no one in any way deceive you [ἐξηπάτησεν], for it [the Day of the Lord] will not come unless the apostasy comes first, and the man of lawlessness is revealed, the son of destruction" (2 Thess. 2:3). Gottleib Lünemann weakens the urgency of Paul's warning by arguing that it should not be interpreted as deliberate, wicked deceit, but only as "a delusion, i.e., of being misled into a false and incorrect mode of contemplation."[20]

The idea of the evil aspect of deception matches the extraordinary character of the period referred to in the remaining verses of 2 Thessalonians 2. In fact, the deception to be avoided is better perceived as the willful and intentional entrapment of unsuspecting victims and may best be represented by the word "beguile."[21] The extended context of 2 Thessalonians 2 gives strong witness to the concept of willful and deliberate deception. This is especially evident in 2:10, where Paul described the man of lawlessness as coming "with all the deception

---

[16] Ibid.

[17] Bauer, Arndt, and Gingrich, *A Greek-English Lexicon of the New Testament and Other Early Christian Literature*, 81-82.

[18] Moulton and Milligan, *The Vocabulary of the Greek Testament*, 57.

[19] This verb, limited to the writings of Paul (Rom. 7:11; 16:18; 1 Cor. 3:18; 2 Cor. 11:3; 1 Tim. 2:14), is regarded as "a strengthened form of ἀπατάω" (Archibald T. Robertson, *Word Pictures in the New Testament* [Nashville: Broadman, 1930, Reprint, Grand Rapids: Baker, n.d.], 6:49). See also Abbott-Smith, *A Manual Greek Lexicon of the New Testament*, 45:208.

[20] Lünemann, *First and Second Thessalonians*, 208.

[21] George G. Findlay, *The Epistles to the Thessalonians*, Cambridge Greek Testament (Cambridge: Cambridge University Press, 1911)166; and Marvin R. Vincent, *Word Studies in the New Testament* (Grand Rapids: Eerdmans, 1946, m 2 --reprint, 4 vols. ,1985), 3:63.

[ἀπάτη]"of wickedness for those who perish." Paul used ἐξαπατάω elsewhere in referring to intentional deception such as the influence of sin (Rom. 7:11), Satan (2 Cor. 11:3; 1 Tim. 2:14), and false teachers (Rom. 16:18).[22] In all the previous cases the deception is intentional and associated with an evil purpose. These very same elements employed by Paul elsewhere in association with this verb will likewise appear in the Tribulation.[23] Thus ἐξαπατάω refers to deliberate intensive deceit.

DECEPTION IN THE TRIBULATION

Prophecies about deception in the Tribulation divide into two categories: statements concerning the coming deception, and warnings to avoid it.

STATEMENTS CONCERNING DECEPTION IN THE TRIBULATION

The Scriptures repeatedly state that deception will be one of the hallmarks of the Tribulation. Jesus' instruction in the Olivet Discourse, Paul's explanation concerning tribulational events, and John's Apocalypse all make multiple references to the massive extent of deception in the Tribulation.

In the Olivet Discourse Jesus instructed His disciples concerning events relevant to His return in glory.[24] He began His discourse on the Tribulation in Matthew 24:4-5 by stating, "See to it that no one misleads you. For many will come in My name, saying, 'I am the Christ and will mislead [πλανήσουσιν] many.'" This warning is expounded in verse 11,

---

[22] Bauer, Arndt, and Gingrich, *A Greek-English Lexicon of the New Testament and Other Early Christian Literature*, 81.

[23] The elements Paul associated with deception can be seen elsewhere in Scripture in reference to deception in the Tribulation: the influence of sin (Matt. 24:12, 21-22), the deception caused by Satan (Rev. 12:9), and the rise of false prophets or false teachers (Matt. 24:12, 24; Rev. 13:11-18).

[24] For discussions of the several interpretational problems pertaining to the chronology of the events predicted in the Olivet Discourse, see George R. Beasley-Murray, *Jesus and the Future* (London: Macmillan, 1954), 12-68; David Wenham, "Recent Studies in Mark 13," *TSF Bulletin* 71 (Spring 1975): 6-15; D. A. Carson, "Matthew," in *The Expositor's Bible Commentary* (Grand Rapids: Eerdmans, 1984), 8:488-95; John F. Walvoord, "Christ's Olivet Discourse on the End of the Age," *Bibliotheca Sacra* 128 (October-December, 1971): 109-16; and idem, *The Prophecy Knowledge Handbook* (Wheaton, IL: Victor, 1990), 380-401.

Satan's Work as a Deceiver

where Jesus stated that "many false prophets will arise and will mislead [πλανήσουσιν] many." Christ later indicated a major means by which the massive deception of the Tribulation will occur: "For false Christs and false prophets will arise and will show great signs and wonders, so as to mislead [πλανῆσαι], if possible, even the elect. Behold, I have told you in advance" (vv. 24-25). From Jesus' words it is evident that deception will occur on a massive scale in the Tribulation, being accomplished by a large number of false Christs and false prophets who will deceive by means of their great signs and wonders.

The apostle Paul also wrote about deception in the Tribulation. In reference to the advent of the man of lawlessness, he described the overall nature of Antichrist's reign not only as being empowered by Satan but also as having as its foremost characteristic the consummation of evil deception. He wrote that the Antichrist will be "the one whose coming is in accord with the activity of Satan, with all power and signs and false wonders, and with all the deception of wickedness [ἐν πάσῃ ἀπάτῃ τῆς ἀδικίας] (2 Thess. 2:9–10a). In verse 11 Paul added that "God will send upon them a deluding influence [ἐνέργειαν πλάνης]". Deception in the Tribulation will be brought about by Satan primarily through the activities of the Antichrist, but also sovereignly supported by a "deluding influence" sent from God.

Besides the deceptive work of the Antichrist, the false prophet will deceive unbelievers. "And he deceives [πλανᾷ] those who dwell on the earth because of the signs which it was given him to perform in the presence of the beast" (Rev. 13:14). And by those signs "he deceived [ἐπλάνησεν] those who had received the mark of the beast and those who worshiped his image" (19:20). Also, in the Tribulation restored Babylon will engage in worldwide deception: "All the nations were deceived [ἐπλανήθησαν] by your sorcery" (18:23).

Then when Christ returns to the earth after the Tribulation, Satan will be bound during the millennium "so that he should not deceive [ἵνα μὴ πλανήσῃ] the nations any longer, until the thousand years were completed; after these things he must be released for a short time" (20:3). At the end of the thousand years Satan will make one final attempt to deceive the world: "And when the thousand years are completed, Satan will be released from his prison, and will come out to deceive [πλανῆσαι] the nations which are in the four corners of the earth" (vv. 7-8). Even when Satan will finally receive his eternal punishment, one additional reference is made to his deception: "And the devil who deceived them [ὁ πλανῶν] was thrown into the lake of fire" (v. 10). While these references to deception refer to activities of Satan after the Tribulation, they still reinforce what a vital role deception plays in his overall character and operations.

By way of summary, the Bible states that a heightened future deception will most assuredly occur during the Tribulation. Those who will accomplish this deception are false Christs (Matt. 24:4-5; Mark 13:5-6), false prophets (Matt. 24:11; Mark 13:22), the Antichrist (Dan. 8:25; 2 Thess. 2:10; 2 John 7), Satan (Rev. 12:9; 20:2-3, 7-8, 10), the false prophet (13:14; 19:20), Babylon (18:23), and God as He sovereignly brings about judgment (2 Thess. 2:11).

WARNINGS CONCERNING THE DECEPTION OF THE TRIBULATION

The statements from Scripture that vast deception will occur during the Tribulation should be sufficient warning for people to be on guard against being engulfed by that deception. Yet along with the repeated statements that such a deception will occur, both Christ and Paul strongly emphasize the need for watchfulness in order to avoid succumbing to the deception of that period.

Denney comments on the weakness of human nature in regard to deception. "Most of us are confident enough of the soundness of our minds, of the solidity of our principles, of the justice of our consciences. It is very difficult for us to understand that we can be mistaken, quite as confident about falsehood as about truth, unsuspecting victims of pure delusion. We can see that some men are in this wretched plight, but that very fact seems to give us immunity. Yet the falsehoods of the last days, St. Paul tells us, will be marvelously imposing and successful. Men will be dazzled by them, and unable to resist."[25] Consequently, a certain

---

[25] James Denney, "The Epistles to the Thessalonians," in *The Expositor's Bible*, ed. W. Robertson Nicoli (New York: A. C. Armstrong and Son, 1903), 22:329-30.

amount of spiritual acumen is needed in order to avoid deception in the present age, let alone in the Tribulation.[26]

In the Olivet Discourse Jesus first responded with a warning to the disciples' questions concerning the events associated with the end times.[27] He began by saying, "See to it [βλέπετε][28] that no one misleads you" (Matt. 24:4). Hiebert underscores the significance of these words: *"Take heed* lays upon them the standing duty to keep their eyes open to the danger of being misled. They must realize that there is the spiritual danger of being misled by religious error. Instead of giving them the sign they had requested (v. 3), Jesus began by alerting them to false signs."[29] As Bruce says, this opening verse in the Olivet Discourse strikes "the practical ethical keynote of the whole discourse: its aim is not to gratify curiosity, but to guard against deception and error."[30] Beasley-Murray notes the repetitive emphasis of βλέπετε in Mark 13. "The disciples were no less open to eschatological suggestion than their fellow Jews (cf. Mark 9:11); an undisciplined desire on their part for signs of the End

---

[26] From a premillennial standpoint the warnings of the Olivet Discourse (Matt. 24-25) relate primarily to the Jews during the Tribulation (as well as Gentiles who will be saved during it). Those warnings can be made applicable to the church only in a general way since the Olivet Discourse presents activities that will occur after the rapture of the church. Application to spiritual alertness on the part of believers during the Church Age must either be along the lines of 1 John 4:1-3, or even more importantly, the repeated warnings for readiness in Revelation 2-3. Spiritual alertness and readiness will be essential for believers who will be saved in the Tribulation as a means of testimony (Luke 21:12-19) as well as prayer (vv. 34-36).

[27] Toussaint cogently argues that the disciples associated the destruction of Jerusalem and the temple with the return of Christ. They thought that what Christ referred to was "completely eschatological" (Stanley D. Toussaint, *Behold the King* [Portland, OR: Multnomah, 198-01, 269-70). So also A. B. Bruce, "The Synoptic Gospels," in *The Expositor's Greek Testament*, ed. W. Robertson Nicoli (Grand Rapids: Eerdmans, 1951), 1:289. Grassmick sees a correspondence between both the destruction of the temple in A.D. 70 and the events in the Great Tribulation at the end of this age. "The 'near' tribulations foreshadowed the 'far' Tribulation of the end time" (John D. Grassmick, "Mark," in *The Bible Knowledge Commentary, New Testament*, ed. John F. Walvoord and Roy B. Zuck [Wheaton, IL: Victor, 1983], 169).

[28] Βλέπετε is often used in the sense of "to consider, look to, take heed" (Abbott-Smith, *A Manual Lexicon of the New Testament*, 83). Paul's similar use of the same word in Philippians 3:2 underscores its significance as a warning.

[29] D. Edmond Hiebert, *Mark, A Portrait of a Servant* (Chicago: Moody, 1974), 317 (italics his).

[30] Bruce, "The Synoptic Gospels," 1:289.

could lead them to give ear to false representations as to the temple, and the Messiah, and the End. Accordingly, 'Beware' is the first, and most needed, word spoken to them. It is also the last (v. 37), and is dominant through all that lies between (vv. 7, 9, 23, 33, 35, 37). The ethical purpose of the revelation is made clear at its commencement."[31]

THE EXTENT OF THE DECEPTION OF THE TRIBULATION

Matthew 24:24-25 records Jesus' warning regarding the great extent of deception that will transpire in the Tribulation: "For false Christs and false prophets will arise and will show great signs and wonders, so as to mislead, if possible, even the elect. Behold, I have told you in advance." The "elect" (vv. 22, 29-31) are Israelites who will survive the Tribulation and enter the kingdom of Christ while still alive. This group will not acknowledge that the Antichrist is God nor will they worship his image. Also, some Gentiles will refuse the demands of the Antichrist, avoid the worldwide deception, follow Jesus, and share in Christ's kingdom glory (vv. 31-40; Dan. 7:14).

Some writers say Matthew 24:24 means the deception of the Tribulation will not be as severe as earlier verses would seem to indicate.[32] However, the verse seems to mean just the opposite, namely, that the elect will initially be susceptible to a certain amount of tribulational deception.[33] For instance, in the phrase "so as to mislead" (ὥστε πλανῆσαι) ὥστε is regularly used with the infinitive to point to an

---

[31] George R. Beasley-Murray, A *Commentary on Mark Thirteen* (London: Macmillan, 1957), 30.

[32] For instance, Hiebert holds that the statement implies the false Christs and false prophets will not succeed in misleading the elect (Hiebert, *Mark, A Portrait of a Servant*, 326). Tasker is even more adamant in his conclusion, stating that false Christs and false prophets "would be powerless to influence God's chosen, however eager they might be to do so" (R. V. G. Tasker, *Matthew*, Tyndale New Testament Commentaries [Grand Rapids: Eerdmans, 1961], 225). Grassmick concludes that the false Christs and false prophets will not succeed in misleading the elect, but he does not explain if any initial deception will take place (Grassmick, "Mark," 170).

[33] The fact that they are designated "elect" indicates that they will ultimately be brought into a saving relationship with Jesus Christ. However, they may initially be deceived along the same lines as those of Titus 3:3 who were deceived before their salvation: "For we also once were foolish ourselves, disobedient, deceived, enslaved to various lusts."

actual result rather than only an intended result.[34] Also, the conditional aspect of εἰ δυνατόν need not rule out the possibility of the elect being temporarily deceived, and it should be viewed as an assumed reality.[35] That even the elect are capable of being initially deceived during the Tribulation reveals the extent of the deception that will occur during that time.[36] However, any deception of the elect will be only temporary and within certain limits.[37] The fact that they are called "the elect" indicates that although they may temporarily reject Christ and possibly be misled by the Antichrist, they ultimately will turn to Christ for their salvation. Consequently, they will not worship the Antichrist as God nor receive "the mark of the beast."[38]

Paul also issued a warning concerning the deception of the Tribulation. As previously noted, Paul began his crucial chapter on the activities of the Antichrist in 2 Thessalonians 2:3 by warning, "Let no

---

[34] Bauer, Arndt, and Gingrich, *A Greek English Lexicon of the New Testament and Other Early Christian Literature,* 899-900. They translate ὥστε ("so that") as in Matthew 27:14: Jesus did not answer Pilate "so that [ὥστε] the governor was quite amazed." Findlay concludes the same by referring ὥστε with the infinitive in 2 Thessalonians 2:4, which presents the actual climactic event of the self-deification of the Antichrist (Findlay, *The Epistles to the Thessalonians,* 169).

[35] H. E. Dana and Julius R. Mantey, *A Manual Grammar of the Greek New Testament* (New York: Macmillan, 1955), 286-88.

[36] While McNeile does not address εἰ δυνατόν in his comments on Matthew 24:24, in his remarks on verse 25, he strongly implies the possibility of the elect being deceived to some degree: "If some of the elect could be deceived, the apostles, being forewarned, should be safe" (Alan Hugh McNeile, *The Gospel according to St. Matthew* [New York: Macmillan, 1915, reprint, Grand Rapids: Baker, 1980], 351).

[37] Bruce seems to emphasize the safety aspect of the elect to such a degree that the deception is greatly diminished, concluding that the teaching of Matthew 24:24 is that the elect cannot be deceived (Bruce, "The Synoptic Gospels," 1:294; so also Robertson, *Word Pictures in the New Testament,* 1:193). Bruce offers as his rationale that if the elect could be deceived at all, "the consequence would be fatal. The 'elect' (who) were selected *for safety* in the evil day—would be involved in general calamity" ("The Synoptic Gospels," 1:294 [italics added]). This conclusion reduces the urgency of Jesus' warning, making it almost superfluous. It could equally be argued that Jesus intended to underscore the vastness of the deception that will occur during that time.

[38] From statements in Revelation 13:16-17 and 14:9-11 it is evident that the deception of the elect is ultimately limited by divine grace. Perhaps such people referred to in Matthew 24:24 may initially think the Antichrist is from God, but will receive the truth (and the true Messiah) later in the Tribulation. If any temporary deception will occur, it obviously will terminate before any of the elect receive the mark of the beast.

one in any way deceive you," and he used the heightened form ἐξαπατήσῃ for "deceive." Although Paul dealt specifically with the Thessalonians' concern that they were in the midst of the Day of the Lord, he still set forth the urgency that they not be misled into error.[39]

Paul predicted the deception of the Tribulation will be "for those who perish, because they did not receive the love of the truth so as to be saved" (2 Thess. 2:10). In other words, unbelievers will be the ones ultimately and totally deceived during the Tribulation.[40] Paul twice made note of the culpability of unbelievers. He viewed their deception as their own choosing "because they did not receive the love of the truth" (v. 10) and they "did not believe the truth, but took pleasure in wickedness" (v. 12). They will be unwilling to come to the truth offered to them and instead will desire to align themselves with wickedness.

John described the extent of the deception by using terms that have worldwide application. In Revelation 3:10 John made use of a term he used ten times in the Apocalypse: "those who dwell upon the earth [τοὺς κατοικοῦντας ἐπὶ τῆς γῆς]."[41] This phrase is consistently used throughout the Apocalypse in reference to the enemies of God who are the objects of His wrath because of their rebellion against Him.[42] These unbelievers will be recipients of deception in the Tribulation. When

---

[39] The only way to avoid the urgency set forth by Paul is to change the entire nature of the epistle. Such is Aus's conclusion, for he contends that in 2 Thessalonians 2:2 the Day of the Lord is synonymous with the "day of the Messiah," which had already come (Roger D. Aus, "The Relevance of Isaiah 66:7 to Revelation 12 and 2 Thessalonians 2," *Zeitschrift fur die neutestamentliche Wissenschaft und die Kunde der Alteren Kirche* 67 [1976], 262). However, Paul's opening statements in verses 1-2 and the explanations in the remainder of the chapter make no sense unless Paul was emphasizing yet future events. For a rebuttal of Aus's position, see Robert L. Thomas, "A Hermeneutical Ambiguity of Eschatology: The Analogy of Faith," *Journal of the Evangelical Theological Society* 23 (March, 1980): 45-53, especially 51-52. Thomas argues that 2 Thessalonians 2:3 refers to events that will happen after the Day of the Lord has begun (and thus would be a source of encouragement for the Thessalonians that they could not have been in the midst of the Day of the Lord).

[40] It is evident that many will be saved during the Tribulation (Rev. 6:9-11; 7:9-17). For a rebuttal of the position that these refer to Christian martyrs of every age and for support that these are martyrs who will have died for the cause of Christ in the Tribulation, see Robert L. Thomas, *Revelation 1-7 An Exegetical Commentary* (Chicago: Moody, 1992), 443-45.

[41] This term is also used in Revelation 6:10; 8:13; 11:10 [twice]; 13:8; 12, 14 [twice]; 17:2, 8.

[42] F. J. A. Hort, *The Apocalypse of St. John* (London: Macmillan, 1908), 35.

Christ returns to the earth He will destroy the false prophet, who will have "deceived those who had received the mark of the beast and those who worshiped his image" (19:20).

This deception of the Tribulation will be worldwide. Only the believing remnant will be devoid of that deception, although some who will ultimately be saved may be temporarily deceived by the Antichrist and the false prophet. In the Tribulation people must either hold allegiance to Christ and will most likely be martyred, or they must align themselves with the forces of Satan.

SUMMARY

The Bible refers a number of times to Satan employing deception in misleading others. This began with his first encounter with mankind in the Garden of Eden and will continue through the current church age. Also, a unique period of unparalleled satanic deception awaits those who will be alive during the Tribulation. Jesus, John, and Paul all made repeated statements about the vast deception that will eventually encompass the entire unbelieving world. Those who adhere to God's Word, although they may be temporarily confused and partially deceived, will avoid the lies of the agents of deception, who will deceive unbelievers, those "who dwell on the earth."

CHAPTER 2

SATAN'S DECEPTIVE MIRACLES IN THE TRIBULATION

Gregory H. Harris

The Bible presents the Tribulation as a unique period whose duration God will limit in order for life to survive (Matt. 24:22). A feature of this unique period is unprecedented works of Satan, whose miracles will be performed in order to deceive many people.

VERSES DEPICTING MIRACULOUS WORKS DURING THE TRIBULATION

Several statements in the Scriptures speak of deception in the Tribulation. This will occur by means of miraculous works performed by some who will be under Satan's leadership.

Jesus made the first reference to miracles in the Tribulation. Having warned about false Christs and false prophets who will arise in His name and mislead many (Matt. 24:4-5, 11), Jesus then indicated the means by which the deception will occur. He prophesied that "false Christs and false prophets will arise and will show great signs and wonders, so as to mislead, if possible even the elect" (v. 24).

A second specific statement about miracles used by forces hostile to God in the Tribulation is in 2 Thessalonians 2:9. Paul described the future "lawless one" (v. 8) as "the one whose coming is in accord with the activity of Satan, with all power and signs and false wonders."

In Revelation 13:14 John wrote, "And he [the second beast] deceives those who dwell upon the earth because of the signs which it was given him to perform in the presence of the beast." This false prophet will continually deceive those who dwell on the earth in the Tribulation. John wrote this about the sixth bowl judgment: "And I saw coming out of the mouth of the dragon and out of the mouth of the beast and out of the mouth of the false prophet, three unclean spirits like frogs; for they are spirits of demons, performing signs, which go out to the kings of the whole world, to gather them together for the war of the great day of God, the Almighty" (16:13-14).

The final reference to the deception of the Tribulation caused by means of the miraculous is Revelation 19:20. When the beast and the false prophet are seized by Christ at His second advent and thrown into the lake of fire, the false prophet is the one "who performed the signs in his [the beast's] presence, by which he deceived those who had the mark of the beast and those who worshiped his image."

WORDS USED TO DESCRIBE THE MIRACLES OF CHRIST AND THE APOSTLES

Before examining the signs and wonders associated with the forces of Satan in the Tribulation, the vocabulary employed in describing the miracles of Christ and the apostles needs to be considered. This provides a base by which the miracles predicted for the Tribulation can be compared, since what is false is best evaluated by what is true.

The Bible employs several words in reference to the miraculous. Thiessen defines a miracle as "a unique and extraordinary event awakening wonder (τέρας), wrought by divine power (δύναμις), accomplishing some practical and benevolent work (ἔργον), and authenticating a messenger and his message as from God (σημεῖον)"[1]

Gregory H. Harris is Associate Professor of Bible Exposition, Southeastern Baptist Theological Seminary, Wake Forest, North Carolina.

[1] Henry C. Theissen, "An Outline of Lectures in Systematic Theology," 3d ed. (class notes,

The word most frequently used of miracles is "sign" (σημεῖον), generally understood as a miracle or supernatural feat.² The word itself indicates that such miracles were never performed randomly and without significance. Instead, a sign was performed "to cause men to respond to the truth confirmed by the sign, to face men with a decision."³ Trench concluded basically the same thing: "But miracles are also σημεῖον. . . . Among all the names which the miracles bear, their ethical end and purpose comes out in σημεῖον with the most distinction, as in τέρας with the least. It is involved and declared in the very word that the prime object and end of the miracle is to lead us to something out of and beyond itself; that, so to speak, it is a kind of fingerpost of God . . . pointing for us to this; valuable, not so much for what it is, as for what it indicates of the grace and power of the doer, or of his immediate connexion [sic] with a higher spiritual world."⁴

The Bible also calls a miracle a "wonder" (τέρας). This word occurs sixteen times in the New Testament, always in the plural, and always linked with σημεῖα.⁵ The combination "signs and wonders" normally denotes supernatural happenings (John 4:48, Acts 2:22, 43; 4:30; 5:12; 6:8; 7:36; 14:3; 15:12; Rom. 15:19; 2 Cor. 12:12; Heb. 2:4).⁶ The word τέρας is "a wonder, marvel,"⁷ "a miracle regarded as a portent or prodigy, awakening amazement . . . and most nearly corresponds, therefore, to the etymological sense of the word miracle."⁸ Pink concludes that τέρας lays

---

Wheaton College, 1942), 9.

² William Hendriksen, *Exposition of I and II Thessalonians,* New Testament Commentary (Grand Rapids: Baker, 1955), 184.

³ Paul Emil Sywulka, "The Contribution of Hebrews 2:3-4 to the Problem of Apostolic Miracles" (Th.M. thesis, Dallas Theological Seminary, 1967), 24.

⁴ Richard C. Trench, *Synonyms of the New Testament* (London: n.p., 1880, reprint, Grand Rapids: Baker, 1953), 342-43.

⁵ Sywulka, "The Contribution of Hebrews 2:3-4 to the Problem of Apostolic Miracles," 25.

⁶ Ernest Best, *A Commentary on the First and Second Epistles to the Thessalonians,* Harper's New Testament Commentaries (New York: Harper and Row, 1972), 305.

⁷ George Abbott-Smith, *A Manual Greek Lexicon of the New Testament,* 3d ed. (Edinburgh: Clark, 1981), 443.

⁸ Marvin R. Vincent, *Word Studies in the New Testament* (New York: Scribner Sons, 1887, reprint, Grand Rapids: Eerdmans, 1946), 1:129.

stress on the effects produced in those who beheld the event,[9] or, as Trench put it, τέρας is "a startling, imposing, amazement-wakening portent or prodigy."[10]

Δύναμις and *ἐνέργεια* occur less frequently. Both point more to the supernatural source rather than to what is produced. *Ἐνέργεια* emphasizes its power in action as distinct from potential power in *δύναμις*.[11] With the exception of 2 Thessalonians 2:9, *ἐνέργεια* is always confined in the New Testament to the workings of God.[12]

These words do not refer to different kinds of miracles as if some were signs, others wonders, and others mighty deeds. They are all used to describe instead "the complete picture of a N. T. miracle."[13] As Hughes notes,

> It is best to take signs, wonders, and miracles as belonging together rather than as indicating three different forms of manifestation. Thus a sign, which is the word consistently used in the Fourth Gospel for the miraculous works of Christ, indicates that the event is not an empty ostentation of power, but is significant in that, signwise, it points beyond itself to the reality of the mighty hand of God in operation. A wonder is an event which, because of its superhuman character, excites awe and amazement on the part of the beholder. A miracle, (or literally power) emphasizes the dynamic character of the event, with particular regard to its outcome or effect.[14]

---

[9] Arthur W. Pink, *An Exposition of Hebrews* (Swengel, PA: Bible Truth, 1954), 2:91.

[10] Trench, *Synonyms of the New Testament*, 341-42.

[11] Walter Grundmann, "ἰσχύω κτλ" in *Theologisches Worterbuch zum Neuen Testament*, ed. Gerhard Kittel (Stuttgart: W. Kohlhammer, 1949), 3:401.

[12] George Milligan, *St. Paul's Epistles to the Thessalonians* (London: Macmillan, 1908), 104. It is significant that 2 Thessalonians describes the man of lawlessness as the one "whose coming is in accord with the activity [ἐνέργειαν] of Satan, with all power and signs and false wonders" (2:9).

[13] Archibald T. Robertson, *A Grammar of the Greek New Testament in the Light of Historical Research* (Nashville: Broadman, 1934), 176. Trench concludes the same thing: "Rather the same miracle is upon one side a *τέρας*, on another a *σημεῖον* and the words most often refer, not to different classes of miracles, but to different qualities in the same miracles" (Trench, *Synonyms of the New Testament*, 341). Stated differently, "They will be found, on closer examination, not so much to represent different kinds of miracles, as miracles contemplated under different aspects and from different points of view" (ibid., 339-40).

[14] Philip Edgcumbe Hughes, *A Commentary on the Epistle to the Hebrews* (Grand Rapids: Eerdmans, 1977), 80-81.

WORDS USED TO DESCRIBE THE MIRACLES OF THE TRIBULATION

Strikingly the words used for the miracles of Christ and the apostles are also used of the miracles performed in the Tribulation by those in allegiance with Satan. Those miracles are called signs (σημεῖον, Rev. 13:13-14; 16:14; 19:20) and the same combination of words is used: great signs and wonders (Matt. 24:24; Mark 13:22), all power and signs and wonders (2 Thess. 2:9). Lenski holds that the "false wonders" (τέρασιν ψεύδους) in 2 Thessalonians 2:9 are not genuinely miraculous. He suggests they are "counterfeit wonders."[15] However, the emphasis placed in the next verses on "deceit" and "the lie" indicate that these should be viewed as miracles leading to the acceptance of the lie associated with the claims of the man of lawlessness.[16] The word ψεῦδος ("false") has to do with the results of the miracles, not with their lack of genuineness[17] or supernatural origin.

Will the satanic miracles in the Tribulation be "magical acts"[18] accomplished by means of ritual incantations? No, they will be genuine miracles, for signs and wonders are always distinct in Scripture from magical activities. For example Simon practiced magic in Samaria (Acts 8:9-11), but Philip performed "signs and great wonders" to the amazement of Simon (v. 13). Also many people in Ephesus who practiced magic repented of their deeds and burned their books related to

---

[15] R. C. H. Lenski, *The Interpretation of St. Paul's Epistles to the Colossians, to the Thessalonians, to Timothy, to Titus and to Philemon* (Minneapolis: Augsburg, 1961), 426.

[16] Charles J. Ellicott, *St. Paul's Epistles to the Thessalonians* (London: Longman, Roberts and Green, 1880), 116.

[17] Robert L. Thomas, "Exegetical Digest of the Epistle of II Thessalonians" (n.p. By the author, 1975), Problem-Solutions section, 92.

[18] Aune defines magic as "ritual procedures for manipulating and coercing supernatural beings for utilitarian ends" (David E. Aune, "The Apocalypse of John and Graeco-Roman Revelatory Magic," *New Testament Studies*, 33 [October, 1987]: 482). He notes papyri with "detailed instructions for the performance of certain ritual acts, the preparation of particular religious paraphernalia and the recitation of prescribed formulas, hymns and prayers, all for use in private (often secret) ceremonies for the achievement of specific goals" (ibid.). While Aune's definition fits the magic of the day, he errs in concluding that "John also mentions the magical feats accomplished by the beast from the earth" (ibid., 494).

practicing magic (19:19).¹⁹ A distinction was made between the miracles God was performing through the hand of Paul ($δυνάμεις$ ... $ὁ\ θεὸς\ ἐποίει$, v. 11) and the rituals of magic concocted by those at Ephesus. These magical activities were never called signs and wonders.²⁰

John referred specifically to signs the false prophet will perform (Rev. 13:13-14; 19:20). Three times in the Apocalypse John made reference to sorceries ($φαρμάκοι$)²¹ that will occur during the Tribulation (9:21; 21:8; 22:15), but nowhere did he identify them with the signs and wonders performed by the Antichrist and the false prophet.

To reduce the miracles of the Tribulation to learned magical activity is unwarranted. Christ Himself designated the miraculous feats that would be performed by false Christs and false prophets as "great signs and wonders" (Matt. 24:24).

THE VERACITY OF THE MIRACLES OF THE TRIBULATION

Does Scripture present these miracles in the Tribulation as authentic miracles, or are they merely counterfeit acts that appear genuine? If they are miraculous, will they differ in any way from the miracles performed by Christ and His apostles? Is it possible that God will grant for a limited time powers that up to now He has reserved for Himself and His select agents? Is God limited in what He can grant Satan and his forces to accomplish? Since the Tribulation is presented as unique from any

---

[19] Paul earlier wrote that magic was a sin that should immediately and totally be removed from the life of a Christian (Gal. 5: 20).

[20] Bacht concludes that false prophets inevitably must rely on magical rites (H. Bacht, "Wahres und falsches Prophetenum," *Biblica* 32 [1951]: 261). While this may be true before the Tribulation, it does not necessarily mean that this will be the case during that time.

[21] The word $φαρμακεία$ occurs frequently in the Septuagint to refer to Egyptian sorceries or to denote poisons, amulets, charms, drugs, magic spells, or any other object supposed to be enchanting (James Glasgow, *The Apocalypse* [Edinburgh: Clark, 1872], 273; James Moffatt, "The Revelation of St. John the Divine," in *The Expositor's Greek Testament*, ed. W. Robertson Nicoli [Grand Rapids: Eerdmans, n.d.], 5:410). The term may be translated "a practice of sorceries" or "witchcraft" (Exod. 7:11; 9:11; Nah. 3:4; Mal. 3:5; Gal. 5:20). (Isbon T. Beckwith, *The Apocalypse of John* [New York: Macmillan, 1919], 570). This form of iniquity is denounced throughout Scripture (Exod. 22:18; Lev. 20:27; Deut. 18:10-12; see also 1 Sam. 28:7; Acts 8:9; 13:8; 19:13-15).

previous time in history, should not unparalleled satanic power be expected, power he has previously been restrained from producing?

Determining the authenticity of the tribulational miracles or the lack thereof will be of tremendous importance in addressing the miraculous components of Revelation 13, the only passage of Scripture that offers any details of what the signs and wonders will be. This determination will also give a clearer understanding of the worldwide deception predicted for that period, since the miraculous is repeatedly presented as the means by which the deception of the Tribulation will occur.

THE VIEW THAT THE TRIBULATION MIRACLES WILL NOT BE AUTHENTIC

Hoekema says Matthew 24:24 "seems to anticipate Paul's description of the antichrist as one who will come 'with pretended signs and wonders' (2 Thess. 2:9)."[22] The New International Version concurs with this interpretation by translating these words in 2 Thessalonians 2:9 as "counterfeit miracles, signs and wonders" instead of authentic miracles.[23] Lenski refers to such deeds as "pretended miracles."[24] He further concludes that Satan is limited to the extent that he can only deceive, but he is unable to perform the supernatural.[25] Robertson says that those who will perform such feats will be skillful charlatans who demonstrate slight-of-hand activities to the excited and gullible masses.[26] Scherrer, who views them as past events, says the miraculous acts presented in

---

[22] Anthony A. Hoekema, *The Bible and the Future* (Grand Rapids: Eerdmans, 1979), 156. Another author acknowledges that the signs and wonders will be the means of deceiving the world at large, as foretold by Daniel, Jesus, Paul, and John, but he does not consider them as actual miracles. Instead these verses convey the principal idea that such a one "will apply his science and philosophy and show that man is extremely powerful" (Herman Hoeksema, *Behold, He Cometh* [Grand Rapids: Reformed Free Publishing Assoc., 1969], 471-72). It is noteworthy that all of Hoeksema's conclusions in this section are based on deduction and conjecture. At no place does he deal with the specifics of the biblical text other than to state what is predicted and then conclude that such things are not possible.

[23] Also the Revised Standard Version (1952 ed.) translates this phrase "with pretended signs and wonders".

[24] Lenski, *The Interpretation of St. Paul's Epistles to the Colossians, to the Thessalonians, to Timothy, to Titus and to Philemon*, 427.

[25] Ibid., 426-27.

[26] A. T. Robertson, *Word Pictures in the New Testament* (Nashville: Broadman, 1933), 1:192.

Revelation 13 were staged theatrics purposely contrived by human means to dupe followers.[27]

Those who say the miracles of the Tribulation will not be authentic must explain two specific signs revealed in Revelation 13, namely, fire called down from heaven (v. 13), and breath being given to the image of the beast (vv. 14-15).

Fire called down from heaven. John recorded that the false prophet will perform "great signs, so that he even makes fire come down out of heaven." Rather than viewing this as a miracle, a number of writers cite similar accounts in the past, accounts that seem to record the miraculous, but which have other plausible explanations. For example, Hippolytus spoke of a sorcerer who could produce a fiery demon that appeared to be called down from heaven before an amazed crowd of worshipers.[28] The sorcerer instructed the audience to cover their eyes as soon as they saw the demon. Hippolytus explained the "miracle" by noting that the sorcerer had a concealed bird previously covered with tow that he would set on fire and release in the room.[29] Another example is from Julius Pollux, who reported a lightning-making device, a piece of equipment used in theaters for special effects.[30] Heron of Alexandria also wrote of a theatrical device that gave the appearance of producing lightning. The "lightning" struck a figure of Ajax, which then immediately vanished from sight. Heron explained that this seeming miracle was accomplished by a rolled-up screen, identical to the stage setting, that was released in an instant in front of the statue, and thus made the statue seem to vanish. What appeared as lightning came through a slit in the ceiling, and on the floor was a board embossed with gold and painted a fiery color.[31]

In each of these references only a semblance of the miraculous occurred. Although many in the audience were deceived, each event had

---

[27] Steven J. Scherrer, "Signs and Wonders in the Imperial Cult: A New Look at a Roman Religious Institution in the Light of Rev. 13:13-15," *Journal of Biblical Literature*, 104 (1984): 600-601.

[28] Hippolytus, *Refutation of All Heresies*, 4:36.

[29] Ibid.

[30] Julius Pollux, *Onomasticon*, 4:130.

[31] Heron of Alexandria, *Druckwerke*, 30:1-6.

a logical explanation with some man-made instrument as its ultimate source. No supernatural element existed, nor was any needed. Some writers conclude that what John viewed in Revelation 13 was the same type of contrived trickery.[32] Yet the biblical text does not present this fire from heaven as trickery.[33]

Giving breath to the image of the beast. In Revelation 13:14-15 John wrote of the second beast (the false prophet): "And he deceives those who dwell on the earth because of the signs which it was given him to perform in the presence of the beast, telling those who dwell on the earth to make an image to the beast who had the wound of the sword and has come to life. And there was given to him to give breath to the image of the beast, that the image of the beast might even speak and cause as many as do not worship the image of the beast to be killed."

Some commentators say that available in John's day were mechanisms that could appear to make an image breathe and speak. Lucian, for example, wrote of Alexander of Abonuteichos, a second-century cultist, who erected a statue of Asclepius in his temple. Lucian described how the statue as having "a serpent head of linen, which had something of a human look, was all painted up, and appeared very lifelike. It would open and close its mouth by means of horse hairs, and a forked black tongue like a snake's, also controlled by horse hairs, would dart out."[34] Lucian described how speech was attributed to the statue:

---

[32] Scherrer concludes that John referred to technology that was available at the time of the writing of the Book of Revelation. Since pagan rituals contain similar accounts where statues appeared to speak and act, all performed by deceptive human invention, John must have referred to similar incidents in Revelation 13 (Scherrer, "Signs and Wonders in the Imperial Cult," 600-601). For a detailed presentation with the same conclusion see Steven J. Scherrer, "Revelation 13 as an Historical Source for the Imperial Cult under Domitian" (Ph.D. diss., Harvard University, 1979), 25-53.

[33] It is rather striking that Scherrer concludes, "We note further that to all indications John himself believes that these were genuine miraculous signs worked through supernatural agency—albeit satanic" ("Signs and Wonders in the Imperial Cult," 600). Even though Scherrer views the events of Revelation 13 as historical occurrences that have already occurred in the early church, he nevertheless affirms that the normal understanding of Revelation 13 indicates that John presented the events as miraculous and not as trickery.

[34] Lucian, *Alexander the False Prophet*, 12.

Again and again, as I said before, he exhibited the serpent to all who requested it, not in its entirety, but exposing chiefly the tail and the rest of the body and keeping the head out of sight under his arm. But as he wished to astonish the crowd still more, he promised to produce the god talking—delivering oracles in person with a prophet. It was no difficult matter for him to fasten cranes' windpipes together and pass them through the head, which he had so fashioned as to be lifelike. Then he answered the questions through someone else, who spoke into the tube from the outside, so that the voice issued from his canvas of Asclepius.[35]

Lucian told how Alexander's deception was accomplished: "Now then, please imagine a little room, not very bright and not admitting too much daylight; also, a crowd of heterogeneous humanity, excited, wonder-struck in advance, agog with hopes. When they went in, the thing, of course, seemed to them a miracle, that the formerly tiny snake within a few days had turned into so great a serpent, with a human face, moreover, and tame! They were immediately crowded towards the exit, and before they could look closely were forced out by those who kept coming in, for another door had been opened on the opposite side as an exit."[36]

Other historical incidents involving the "activities" of statues are considered comparable to what John described. Hippolytus told of a skull made out of wax that appeared to be able to speak through tubes constructed from "the windpipe of a crane."[37] The wax skull could even be made to disappear before the very eyes of the worshipers by simply preparing coals, as if for incense, which would melt the wax when it was placed close to it.[38] Athenaeus described a massive procession where a statue of Dionysus's nurse, Nysa, was transported before the multitudes "After these women came a four-wheeled cart twelve feet wide and drawn by sixty men, in which was seated an image of Nysa, twelve feet high; she had on a yellow tunic with gold spangles, and was in a Laconian shawl. Moreover, this image could rise up automatically

---

[35] Ibid., 26.

[36] Ibid., 16.

[37] Hippolytus, *Refutation of All Heresies*, 4:41.

[38] Ibid.

without anyone putting his hands to it, and after pouring a libation of milk from a gold saucer it would sit down again."[39]

Others hold that the fire called down from heaven, though not a reflection of a past event, is a "pseudo-miracle,"[40] which will be performed through a relatively moderate skill in pyrotechnics.[41] The giving of breath to the image, however, is considered of even greater import and consequently not available for Satan's agents to perform. Walvoord expresses this view: "Expositors usually hold that the extraordinary powers given by Satan to the false prophet do not extend to giving life to that which does not possess life, because this is a prerogative of God alone. The intent of the passage seems to be that the image has the appearance of life manifested in breathing, but actually it may be no more than a robot. The image is further described as being able to speak, a faculty easily accomplished by mechanical means."[42]

In this and similar views the deceptive acts in the Tribulation, then, are considered tricks that appear miraculous. However, there are several problems with this. For one thing all the historical examples cited were contrived by different individuals and with limited influence, whereas the deception by the false prophet will be worldwide and the work of one individual (Rev. 13:12, 14, 16; 19:20).[43] Nor were they of such magnitude "so as to mislead, if possible, even the elect" (Matt. 24:24). Non-Christian witnesses readily identified the means by which a mechanical device worked, and they were not deceived. Also, the ability to perform Tribulation miracles will be given ($\dot{\varepsilon}\delta\dot{o}\theta\eta$) to the false prophet (Rev. 13:14-15), but in magical feats nothing is "given" to its perpetrators by

---

[39] Athenaeus, *The Deipnosophistae*, 5:198. Again the mechanics and an explanation are not detailed by the author, perhaps because no close examination of the statue was permitted. As with the other examples, the deception was quite isolated and did not provoke worldwide amazement.

[40] George E. Ladd, A *Commentary on Revelation* (Grand Rapids: Eerdmans, 1972), 184.

[41] Moses Stuart, *A Commentary on the Apocalypse* (Edinburgh: Maclachan, Stewart, 1847), 647.

[42] John F. Walvoord, *The Revelation of Jesus Christ* (Chicago: Moody, 1966), 208.

[43] Scherrer concludes that the historical references he cites indicate that technology existed "that could be very effectively used to make quite an impression on the worshipers" (Scherrer, "Signs and Wonders in the Imperial Cult," 601). However, the Revelation account extends to all the unbelieving world, not to a select few previously aligned with an established imperial cult.

which they deceive their audiences. A mechanical device or invention does not qualify as a "great sign" in the miraculous sense.

THE VIEW THAT THE TRIBULATION MIRACLES WILL BE AUTHENTIC

Several factors indicate that the miracles of the Tribulation will be authentic and unexplainable by any human measures.

First, since the Tribulation will be a unique period of time (Matt. 24:21-22), comparisons between satanic counterfeits during the present church age or before and the miracles predicted for the Tribulation should be minimized. As was noted, exactly the same words used for the miracles of Christ and the apostles are used in reference to the miracles of the Tribulation. To say that the signs, wonders, and mighty deeds attributed to Satan's forces will only seem to be miraculous could lead to questioning the veracity of the miracles of Christ, since one could say that they too only seemed to be miraculous.

Second, God will grant authority to the Antichrist and the false prophet to perform miracles in the Tribulation. If Satan alone will empower his two agents, then they may very well be limited in their abilities and may only appear to perform the miraculous. On the other hand, if it can be shown that God will grant authority to the Antichrist and the false prophet, then the authenticity of their miracles becomes much more feasible.

A distinction exists between the meaning of the words "power" (δύναμις) and "authority" (ἐξουσία). Δύναμις refers to "any potential strength based on inherent physical, spiritual, or natural powers, and is exhibited in spontaneous actions, powerful deeds, and natural phenomena."[44] Therefore, the Lord God and the Lamb are uniquely worthy "to receive glory and honor and power [δύναμιν]" (Rev. 4:11) and "to receive power [δύναμιν] and riches and wisdom and might and honor and glory and blessing" (5:12). These components are innately God's. On the other hand ἐξουσία "denotes the power which may be

---

[44] Otto Betz, *"ἐξουσία,"* in *The New International Dictionary of New Testament Theology*, ed. Colin Brown, trans. G. H. Boobyer et al. (Grand Rapids: Zondervan, 1976), 2:607.

displayed in the areas of legal, political, social, or moral affairs."[45] Authority is "always linked with a particular position or mandate; so that it refers to the right of a king, a father or a tenant to dispose as he wishes."[46] $Δύναμις$ relates more to innate power or capacity to perform certain activities, while $ἐξουσία$ has reference to the realm of influence within which one may operate.

The Book of Revelation maintains this distinction. In 13:2 Satan will give the Antichrist his power ($δύναμιν αὐτοῦ$),[47] something also attested to in 2 Thessalonians 2:9. Nowhere does the Bible say God will empower the Antichrist, although as a created being, whatever power he exercises ultimately comes from God.[48]

Authority ($ἐξουσία$), on the other hand, will be given by God on several occasions in the Tribulation. With all authority belonging to the Godhead (Matt. 28:18-19), any authority exercised, including that of Satan, is ultimately derived from God. God will give authority ($ἐξουσία$) to Death and Hades to destroy over a fourth of the earth (Rev. 6:8). The two witnesses likewise will be given authority to prevent rain from falling, authority over the waters to turn them to blood, and authority to smite the earth with every plague (11:6). Even demonic beings released from the abyss will be granted authority to inflict punishment on the unredeemed during the Tribulation (9:3-4). Consequently, both agents of God and agents of evil will receive certain authority from God in the Tribulation in accord with His purpose.

It is evident in Scripture that Satan will play a dominant role in both empowering and granting authority to the Antichrist and false prophet. Second Thessalonians 2:9 tells of "the one whose coming is in accord

---

[45] Ibid. An aspect of this is seen in that $ἐξουσία$ is derived from $ἔξεστιν$, "it is possible, it is permitted, it is allowed. The word came to denote "unrestricted possibility or freedom of action" or "right of action" (ibid., 606). Of course not all authority is the same, the parameters under which a given authority operates differ greatly.

[46] Ibid., 607.

[47] The only other instance in the Book of Revelation in which the Antichrist receives power ($δύναμις$) occurs in 17:13, which says the ten kings will "give their power and authority to the beast".

[48] Werner Foerster, "$ἔξεστιν κτλ$" in *Theological Dictionary of the New Testament*, ed. Gerhard Kittel, trans. Geoffrey W. Bromiley (Grand Rapids: Zondervan, 1964), 2:567.

with the activity of Satan, with all power [πάσῃ δυνάμει] and signs and false wonders." Additional evidence is seen in Revelation 13:2, where John recorded that "the dragon gave him [the beast] his power [δύναμιν] and his throne and great authority [ἐξουσίαν]." Verse 4 indicates that the unbelieving world at large will "worship the dragon because he gave his authority [ἐξουσίαν] to the beast." And the false prophet will "exercise all the authority [ἐξουσίαν] of the first beast in his presence" (v. 12). Since Satan will give great authority to the first beast, and the second beast will exercise the same power as the first, then Satan must also give power to the second beast.

That Satan will give his authority to both the Antichrist and the false prophet is significant in determining the veracity of tribulational miracles, particularly in reference to fire being called down from heaven. God permitted Satan to afflict Job, stating, "Behold, all that he has is in your power, only do not put forth your hand on him" (Job 1:12). In this case God granted authority to Satan, but He also limited that authority. One of the calamities inflicted on Job is described in 1:16: "While he [a messenger] was still speaking, another also came and said, 'The fire of God fell from heaven and burned up the sheep and the servants and consumed them, and I alone have escaped to tell you.'" Whether the fire of God was lightning similar to that recorded in 1 Kings 18:38[49] or combined with brimstone similar to Genesis 19:24[50] need not be determined for this study. What is significant is that although the fire from heaven was attributed to God by the messenger, Satan was the sending agent.[51] Satan was able to call fire from heaven of such

---

[49] Roy B. Zuck, "Job," in *The Bible Knowledge Commentary, Old Testament*, ed. John F. Walvoord and Roy B. Zuck (Wheaton, IL: Victor, 1985), 720.

[50] Stanley Leathes, "Job," in *Ellicott's Commentary on the Whole Bible*, ed. Charles John Ellicott (Grand Rapids: Zondervan, n.d.), 4:8.

[51] Smick concludes the term "fire of God"... does not mean God is considered the immediate source, but is simply phenomenal language (Elmer B. Smick, "Job," in *The Expositor's Bible Commentary*, ed. Frank E. Gaebelein [Grand Rapids: Zondervan, 1988], 4:883). A similar example is those who described Simon Magus as possessing "the Great Power of God" (Acts 8:10). The accuracy is in the recording of what the people concluded, not in the content of their statement. Interestingly, Simon Magus requested authority (ἐξουσία), not power (δύναμις), to perform the same works Peter and John performed (Acts 8:19).

The Lie

magnitude as to destroy seven thousand sheep and their keepers. Obviously no human element can explain this supernatural act.

This event in Job 1 shows that in certain instances God may grant Satan authority to act beyond his normal realm of operation. Since Satan in the Tribulation will give his authority to the first beast (Rev. 13:2, 4) and subsequently to the second beast (v. 12), it would be expected that Satan's agents will likewise have authority to call down fire from heaven, something Scripture designates as a "great sign" (v. 13), and a major component of tribulational deception (v. 14).

Third, while Satan is limited in that he can do only what God permits, God will add to the capabilities of Satan and his agents in an unprecedented and greatly expanded manner. This too lends support to the veracity of the Tribulation miracles.

Initial support is seen in that the Antichrist will receive a victor's crown ($\sigma\tau\acute{\epsilon}\phi\alpha\nu o\varsigma$)[52] at the breaking of the first seal in Revelation 6:1-2. This seal judgment obviously will originate from God, as the Son alone is found worthy to break the seals on the scroll and to start the Tribulation judgments. In fact, all the events of this section of the Apocalypse are initiated from the throne of God introduced in Revelation 4.[53] In addition, Satan will play no part in the breaking of the first seal and the bringing forth of the rider on the white horse. So while Satan will give the Antichrist his power, throne, and great authority in Revelation 13, God will also broaden the domain of the Beast by giving him imperial dignity at the beginning of his activity and before any of his conquests occur.[54] While this event alone does not address the miracles

---

[52] Because $\sigma\tau\acute{\epsilon}\phi\alpha\nu o\varsigma$ often refers to a symbol of conquest and even to conquest of good over evil, some hold that it must be applied to something that reflects ultimate victory (Charles, *The Revelation of St. John*, 1:163; Ladd, *A Commentary on the Revelation of John*, 97). However, the broader context, especially Revelation 4-5, indicates that the crown is that of a victor, not of a sovereign (Walvoord, *The Revelation of Jesus Christ*, 127). While the victory can be on a grand scale, it need not be the ultimate victory.

[53] E. W. Bullinger, *The Apocalypse or "The Day of the Lord"* (London: Eyre and Spottiswoode, n.d.), 255.

[54] Walter Scott, *Exposition of the Revelation of Jesus Christ* (Swengel, PA: Bible Truth, n.d.), 147.

predicted for the Tribulation, it does add credence to God's granting authority to the Antichrist.

As noted earlier, God's hand in the activities of the Antichrist and the false prophet is seen in the repeated use of ἐδόθη throughout the Book of Revelation. From the root δίδωμι, this verb is frequently employed in the sense of granting what would otherwise be unattainable through one's own efforts, especially as seen in what is given by God Himself. This is true both in the Gospel of John and the Book of Revelation. Two verses in particular show this. John 6:65 states, "No one can come to Me, unless it has been granted [δεδομένον] him from the Father." In reference to Pilate's authority (ἐξουσίαν), Jesus answered that Pilate "would have no authority . . . unless it had been given [δεδομένον] . . . from above" (19:11). In the Book of Revelation the aorist passive form ἐδόθη bears the same connotation. It repeatedly occurs in reference to a special prerogative or capacity God grants a person or being.[55] For instance, three riders on the horses of the first four seal judgments were given, respectively, a victor's crown (Rev. 6:2), authority to take peace from the earth (v. 4), and authority to kill over a fourth of the earth (v. 8). The martyrs described in the fifth seal were given a white robe from God (v. 11). The angels standing at the four corners of the earth were granted to harm the earth and the sea (7:1-2). When John viewed the breaking of the seventh seal, he saw seven angels who were given trumpets to be used as part of God's wrath against the world (8:1-2). In this same scene a golden censer representing the prayers of the saints was given to another angel (8:3-4). The fifth angel sounded a trumpet which brought forth a star from heaven who was given the key to the bottomless pit (9:1).[56] John was given a measuring rod to measure the temple of God (11:1).[57] The future tense δώσω is used in reference to the authority God

---

[55] Robert L. Thomas, "Exegetical Digest of Revelation 4-7" (n.p. By the author, 1987), 159.

[56] Thomas discusses eight views on the identity of this star from heaven ("Exegetical Digest of Revelation 8-14," 51-57). Based on the similarities with the angel of Revelation 20:1, who comes down from heaven with the key to the abyss, many see this as a reference to an unfallen angel used specifically for this task by God (e.g., Beckwith, *The Apocalypse of John*, 560, and Mounce, *The Book of Revelation*, 192-93).

[57] God's command that measurements be made is also given in regard to Jerusalem (Zech. 2:1-2), the future temple (Ezek. 40-42), and the New Jerusalem (Rev. 21:15-17). The act of

will grant His two witnesses (11:3), but the same sense still applies.[58] In Revelation 12:14 reference is made to two wings given to the woman to escape the dragon. The fourth angel of the bowl judgments "poured out his bowl upon the sun; and it was given to it to scorch men with fire" (16:8). In describing the participants of the marriage supper of the Lamb, John wrote that "it was given to her to clothe herself in fine linen" (19:8). A final use of ἐδόθη in the Book of Revelation occurs in reference to the participants of the millennial kingdom: "And I saw thrones, and they sat upon them, and judgment was given to them" (20:4). In all these instances God grants special privileges or capacities that are unattainable through the individual's efforts. In each instance the granting of such capacities serves either a designated function of God's sovereign design or else a special privilege or reward.

While it is expected that God would grant special capabilities to His own select agents, the consistent use of ἐδόθη in the Book of Revelation also indicates that God will do this even to those aligned against Him. The demons who ascend out of the bottomless pit are given authority (καὶ ἐδόθη αὐταῖς ἐξουσία) to torment those who do not follow God (9:3-4). Although Revelation 9:5 in the New American Standard Bible states that those demons "were not permitted to kill anyone," a literal translation is, "and it was given to them not to kill anyone [καὶ ἐδόθη αὐτοῖς ἵνα μὴ ἀποκτείνωσιν]." In this case God not only granted authority but also placed restrictions on their activities and time allotment. The context of Revelation 9 demonstrates that God alone is the One who gives such special abilities even to demonic forces since this will take place as part of the fifth trumpet judgment, something in which Satan has no active role. In addition to this, it is most doubtful that Satan would limit the activity of these demons to five months (v. 5), as well as restrict their mission of torment so that those faithful to God will not be affected (v. 4).

---

measuring seems to be an indication of what belongs to God in some special capacity. God is seen as evaluating His property (Walvoord, *The Revelation of Jesus Christ*, 176).

[58] The future tense may be employed here because John was hearing at this point what would transpire (Rev. 11:1-3). To hear what would take place, instead of seeing it, was needed to express the God-ordained time limitations within the verses.

Another instance of God's granting special prerogatives for those aligned against Him is seen in the temple being given to the nations who will tread it under foot for forty-two months (11:2). Satan would have no authority over the temple unless God granted it, especially since it is specifically designated as "the temple of God" (v. 1). Also, as stated before, if Satan is the one who gives the authority for the temple to be trodden down, one may ask why he would limit this abuse to only forty-two months. Much more reasonable is the conclusion, as with the other examples throughout the Book of Revelation, that ἐδόθη signifies a privilege or capacity granted by God by which He authorizes something that would otherwise be unattainable. Also, important to note is the fact that God may place time limits on what will be granted. Granting special capabilities, especially to evil agents, does not mean that these abilities are theirs to use indefinitely and indiscriminately.

Six times Revelation 13 uses ἐδόθη in reference to some specific authority given to the Antichrist (vv. 5 [twice], 7 [twice]),[59] as well as to the miracles given the false prophet to perform (vv. 14-15). To the Antichrist was given (a) a mouth that spoke arrogant words and blasphemies, (b) authority (ἐξουσία) to act for forty-two months, (c) the capacity to make war with the saints and to overcome them, and (d) authority over every tribe, people, tongue, and nation. The false prophet was given signs to perform to deceive those who dwell on the earth (v. 14) and "there was given to him to give breath to the image of the beast" (v. 15).

Some say the authority given to the Antichrist and false prophet in 13:5 and 7 was given by Satan,[60] but it seems preferable to view this as authority granted by God because of the repeated use of ἐδόθη and the similarities with God's activities recorded earlier in the book. For

---

[59] In the Greek text ἐδόθη begins each clause, thus emphasizing the fact that these capabilities will be given and not be part of his innate being. Such a designation differs vastly from the innate characteristics of Jesus presented in Revelation 1-5.

[60] While noting that the vast majority of times ἐδόθη refers ultimately to power given by God, some choose to apply it in Revelation 13:3-4 to authority given by Satan (Swete, *The Apocalypse of St. John*, 165; and Robertson, *Word Pictures in the New Testament*, 6:400). Neither author gives any support for this conclusion, nor do they cite any other instance in the Book of Revelation where ἐδόθη is used in any manner other than for that which is granted by God.

instance, God empowers the demons from the bottomless pit (9:3, καὶ ἐδόθη αὐταῖς ἐξουσία), so there is precedent for God granting special authority even to agents of Satan. Since God limits the time frame and parameters of Satan's activities, it is not surprising that He would do the same with Satan's chief agents in the Tribulation. Satan will empower his special agents (13:4), but God will add to and broaden their authority, authorizing the Antichrist temporarily to exercise unprecedented power over the world (vv. 5-9).

Consistent with the multiple uses of ἐδόθη throughout the Book of Revelation, this term signifies what is granted by God alone and not by Satan. Therefore, the miracles detailed in Revelation 13 should be viewed as authentic miracles.

Fourth, the authenticity of the coming tribulational miracles is seen in the extensive deception that will be carried out by the false prophet, whom John described as the one "who performed the signs in his [i.e., the beast's] presence, by which he deceived those who had received the mark of the beast" (19:20). The primary means of deception will come about by miraculous signs the false prophet will perform. He will deceive all who will receive the mark of the beast, that is, the entire unbelieving world.[61] Therefore, what will be performed must be beyond the grasp of any technical explanation.

Fifth, Jesus predicted that "false Christs and false prophets will arise and show great signs and wonders, so as to mislead, if possible, even the elect" (Matt. 24:24). Jesus called special attention to this fact in His next statement: "Behold,[62] I have told you in advance" (v. 25). The importance of what Jesus predicted, especially in reference to the great signs and wonders of the Tribulation, should not be diminished in any way, since He called special attention to it.

---

[61] The false prophet will deceive "those who received the mark of the beast and those who worshiped his image" (Rev. 19:20; cf. 13:16; 14:9-11; 16:2; 20:4) (Robertson, *Word Pictures in the New Testament*, 6:455).

[62] Aune notes that "Behold" (ἰδού) occurs in strategic passages to alert the reader as to the cruciality of what is about to be said, it arrests the attention of the reader (David Aune, *Prophecy in Early Christianity and the Ancient Mediterranean* [Grand Rapids: Eerdmans, 1983], 279).

CONCLUSION

The miracles of the Tribulation will be authentic miracles, not merely actions that seem miraculous. They will be genuine, not counterfeit. The false prophet will be granted the capability to call fire down from heaven and to give breath to the image of the beast. Other authentic miracles will also be performed, though the Bible does not identify these other than referring to them as "great signs" (Rev. 13:13; cf. Matt. 24:24) and "signs" (Rev. 16:13-14). John limited the activity of the image to speaking, especially in regard to sentencing to death those who will not worship it (13:15). The view that unprecedented demonic activity beyond current conditions should be expected during the Tribulation harmonizes with the release of demons who are presently bound in the abyss (9:1-11). That the statue will actually speak, and not merely seem to speak, accords with the biblical text. Such an act would qualify as a genuine miraculous sign without human invention or mechanism. It would also qualify as a special capacity "given" [$\dot{\varepsilon}\delta\acute{o}\theta\eta$] to the false prophet to perform, something he would be incapable of doing unless power was given to him, even beyond the authority that Satan will give him. Such an unexplainable sign would also accomplish the worldwide deception on the lost world that John predicted would take place as a result.

CHAPTER 3

DOES GOD DECEIVE?
THE "DELUDING INFLUENCE"
OF SECOND THESSALONIANS 2:11

*Gregory H. Harris**

*S*cripture uses several Greek and Hebrew words to denote deception, particularly in relation to the future period of Tribulation. Second Thess. 2:11 is of special interest in discussions of deception during that future time, because God is the agent who sends the "deluding influence" (energeian planēs) among unbelievers. Two OT passages which present God as in some way deceiving are analogous to God's future activity of this kind, 1Kgs. 22:22 and Ezek. 14:9. Romans 1:18-32 is partially parallel to that future action. Just as divine judgment of the rebellious was at the heart of God's deceptive activity in the two OT examples, so it will be during the future Tribulation. His judgment on a rebellious world will take many forms with deception being only one of them. In all cases of His use of deception, He exposes falsehood by presenting His truth. His particular opponent in the future will be "the man of lawlessness" (2 Thess. 2:3) who will offer "the lie" (2 Thess. 2:11) in place of the truth. This agent of evil will have a very wide

---

* Professor Harris is Associate Professor of Bible Exposition at Southeastern Baptist Theological Seminary, Wake Forest, North Carolina.

following because of his use of deceptive methods. God will then add to the deception of this man's followers by sending them the "deluding influence" that will move them beyond the possibility of receiving the truth.

* * * * *

PRELIMINARY CONSIDERATIONS REGARDING DECEPTION

From the earliest deception of Eve in Genesis 3 up through Satan's final attempt to deceive the world in Revelation 20, deception has played a significant role in the history of man. It is fitting that Scripture presents Satan at both the first and last efforts to deceive mankind, because ultimately all religious deception is traceable to Satan, "the serpent of old . . . who deceives the whole world" (Rev. 12:9).[1] Multiple verses in Scripture bear witness of this, such as John 8:44, which states of Satan, "Whenever he speaks a lie, he speaks from his own nature, for he is a liar, and the father of lies."[2] Two other verses specifically identify Satan's role as a deceiver, especially in regard to the fall of man. In 2 Cor. 11:3 Paul warned, "But I am afraid, lest as the serpent deceived Eve by his craftiness, your minds should be led astray from the simplicity and purity of devotion to Christ." In an even more succinct statement, Paul later wrote in 1 Tim. 2:14, "[I]t was not Adam who was first deceived, but the woman being quite deceived, fell into transgression."

Deception, at its core, is a lie in place of the truth. The NT words repeatedly used for deception, πλανάω (*planaō*) and ἀπατάω (*apataō*), bear this out.[3] The two words are used interchangeably throughout

---

[1] Scripture quotations are from the 1971 ed. of the New American Standard Bible.

[2] For a discussion of other references to Satan's deception, see this writer's article, "Satan's Work as a Deceiver," *Bibliotheca Sacra* 156 (April-June 1999): 190-202.

[3] The OT contains surprisingly little in regard to the deceptive work of Satan. In fact, the OT presents relatively few verses on Satan (D. Edmond Hiebert, "Satan," in *Zondervan Pictorial Encyclopedia of the Bible*, ed. Merrill C. Tenney [Grand Rapids: Zondervan, 1975], 5:282). Many of the events of satanic deception are later revealed in the NT. Only one passage specifically links tribulational deception to the Antichrist. Daniel 8:25 reads, "And through his shrewdness he will

Scripture and seem to have no major distinction between them.[4] The verb *planaō* is rendered "to cause to wander, lead astray,"[5] or "to lead astray, mislead by means of deception."[6] The passive voice conveys the idea, "to let oneself be misled, deceived."[7] The noun derivative "deception" (πλάνη, *planē*) means, "wandering from the path of truth, error, delusion, deceit, deception to which one is subject."[8] That satanic deception always stands in contrast to the standard of God's revelatory truth is of utmost importance.[9] The other Greek verb for deception, *apataō*, does not occur as frequently in the NT as *planaō*, but it likewise conveys the idea of deceiving, cheating, or misleading someone.[10] An intensified derivative (ἐξαπατάω, *exapataō*) expresses a strengthened form of deception.[11]

The Bible repeatedly uses both words for Satan's activities of deception in history past as well as for the deception associated with the

---

cause deceit to succeed by his influence." The Hebrew word used here is מִרְמָה, from the verb stem רָמָה. The root carries the sense of "beguile, deceive, mislead." It occurs repeatedly in regard to treacherous or deceitful speech and is never used in any kind of positive manner (William White, "רמה," in *Theological Wordbook of the Old Testament*, ed. R. Laird Harris, Gleason L. Archer, Jr., and Bruce K. Waltke, vol. 2 [Chicago: Moody, 1980]: 849; so also Francis Brown, S. R. Driver, and Charles A. Briggs, *A Hebrew and English Lexicon of the Old Testament*, trans. Edward Robinson [Oxford: At the Claredon Press, 1959], s.v. "רָמָה" 941).

[4] G. B. Winer, *Grammar Idiom of the New Testament*, trans. J. Henry Thayer (Andover, Mass.: Flagg and Gould, 1825; reprint, Andover, Mass.: Draper, 1970), 500.

[5] George Abbott-Smith, *A Manual Lexicon of the New Testament* (Edinburgh: Clark, 1952), 363.

[6] Henry George Liddell and Robert Scott, *A Greek-English Lexicon*, 9th ed., rev. Henry Stuart Jones (Oxford: Clarendon, 1940), 2:1411.

[7] Walter Bauer, William F. Arndt, and F. Wilbur Gingrich, *A Greek-English Lexicon of the New Testament and Other Early Christian Literature*, 2d ed., rev. F. Wilbur Gingrich and Frederick W. Danker (Chicago: University of Chicago, 1979), 665. Compare this use of the passive in Matt. 24:24; Luke 21:8; John 7:47; Rev. 18:23.

[8] Ibid., 671.

[9] Lünemann, "First and Second Thessalonians," in *Meyer's Critical and Exegetical Commentary on the New Testament* (Edinburgh: Clark, 1880), 46. For more detail on this important aspect of satanic deception, see Harris, "Satan's Work as a Deceiver," 193-96.

[10] Bauer, Arndt, and Gingrich, *A Greek-English Lexicon of the New Testament and Other Early Christian Literature*, 81-82.

[11] Archibald T. Robertson, *Word Pictures in the New Testament* (Nashville: Broadman, 1930; reprint, Grand Rapids: Baker, n.d.), 6:49. For the various uses of this word throughout Scripture, see Harris, "Satan's Work as a Deceiver," 195-96.

future Tribulation. In fact, the Tribulation will be a time of satanic deception unlike any other in history. As bad as Satan's previous deceptions have been, it will pale in comparison to what awaits the world ahead. Every major NT passage that details events and persons operative during the Tribulation (Matthew 24–25/Mark 13; 2 Thessalonians 2; Revelation 4–20) presents statements and warnings about tribulational deception.[12] Both Greek words for deception occur repeatedly, with forms of *planaō* occurring more in Revelation than in any other NT book.[13] In fact, not only does the Bible predict a greatly intensified deception during the Tribulation, it also discloses the agents of that deception. Specific agents of deception will be false Christs (Matt. 24:4-5; Mark 13:5-6), false prophets (Matt. 24:11; Mark 13:22), the Antichrist (Dan. 8:25; 2 Thess. 2:10; 2 John 7), Satan (Rev. 12:9; 20:2-3, 7-8, 10), the false prophet (13:14; 19:20), Babylon (18:23), and in a completely different sense to be discussed below, God (2 Thess. 2:11).[14]

THE CONTROVERSY OVER 2 THESS. 2:11

That Scripture predicts deception of the unbelieving world during the Tribulation is not surprising, especially in light of Satan's past history. However, 2 Thess. 2:11-12 introduces an unexpected party associated with deception during that period: "And for this reason God will send upon them a deluding influence so that they might believe what is false, in order that they all may be judged who did not believe the truth, but took pleasure in wickedness." The "deluding influence" (ἐνέργειαν πλάνης, *energeian planēs*) is highly controversial and has caused much debate. A striking aspect is the linking of the same word used elsewhere for satanic deception (*planaō*) with a work of God. In fact, with the exception of 2 Thess. 2:11, every other Scripture predicting tribulational deception attributes the deception to Satan and his agents. Second

---

[12] For a detailed analysis of the statements and warnings see this writer's "The Theme of Deception During the Tribulation" (Th.D. dissertation, Dallas Theological Seminary, May 1998), 20-28.

[13] Robert L. Thomas, *Revelation 1–7: An Exegetical Commentary* (Chicago: Moody, 1992), 12.

[14] Harris, "Satan's Work as a Deceiver," 197.

Thessalonians depicts the man of lawlessness as coming in accord with "the activity of Satan" (2:9), as well as with "all the deception of wickedness" (2:10). One would expect a continuation of Satan's role in empowering such a person. Instead, Paul switches to God as the sender of the *energeian planēs*. To associate God with any form of deception is unusual; one should approach this verse cautiously.

Multiple questions emerge because of this verse. Does 2 Thess. 2:11 present God as the source for any deception predicted for the Tribulation? If so, this has theological consequences. For instance, does God actively deceive? If God deceives, then one who is judged by God can blame God for his sinful actions, since God deceived him. Such reasoning carried to its logical conclusion would lead to the biblically untenable conclusion that God is a liar—since deception at its core is a lie—and that God is the author of sin. Because of these and other related questions, examining 2 Thess 2:11 in regard to tribulational deception is essential.[15]

Though the previous questions concerning God and the deception of the Tribulation are pertinent, they should not detract from the core truth

---

[15] For discussions and views on theodicy, including God's use of intermediary agents of evil, see John Hick, *Evil and the Love of God* (New York: Harper and Row, 1966); Jacques Maritain, *God and the Permission of Evil* (Milwaukee, Wis.: Bruce Publishing Co., 1966); Frederick Sontag, *Why Did You Do That?* (Philadelphia: Westminster, 1970); Henry John McCloskey, *God and Evil* (The Hague: Nijhoff Publishers, 1974); Alvin Plantinga, *God, Freedom, and Evil* (New York: Harper and Row, 1974); David Griffin, *God, Power, and Evil: A Process Theodicy* (Philadelphia: Westminster 1976); W. Sibley Towner, *How God Deals With Evil* (Philadelphia: Westminster, 1976); Philip Edgcumbe Hughes, *Hope for a Despairing World: The Christian Answer to the Problem of Evil* (Grand Rapids: Baker, 1977); S. Paul Schilling, *God and Human Anguish* (Nashville: Abingdon, 1977); Bruce R. Reichenbach, *Evil and a Good God* (New York: Fordham University, 1982); James L. Crenshaw, *Theodicy in the Old Testament* (Philadelphia: Fortress, 1983); Michael L. Peterson, *Evil and the Christian God* (Grand Rapids: Baker, 1982); Dan R. Stiver, "The Problem of Theodicy," *Review and Expositor* 93 (Fall 1996): 507-17; Albert W. J. Harper, "The Theodicy of Suffering," *Scripta Theologica* 28 (Summer 1996): 103; James A. Keller, "The Hiddenness of God and the Problem of Evil," *International Journal for Philosophy of Religion* 37 (Fall 1995): 13-24; Terrence W. Tilley, "The Evils of Theodicy," *Scripta Theologica* 26 (January-April 1994): 338-39; Daniel B. Clendenin, "God is Great, God is Good: Questions About Evil," *Ashland Theological Journal* 24/35-54 (1992): 35-54; William Hasker, "Providence and Evil: Three Theories," *Religious Studies* 28 (March 1992): 91-105; William Hasker, "The Necessity of Gratuitous Evil," *Faith and Philosophy* 9 (January 1992): 23-44; Grant R. Osborne, "Theodicy in the Apocalypse," *Trinity Journal* 14 (Spring 1993): 63-77.

of 2 Thess. 2:11: *God* will send the deluding influence in the Tribulation. Whatever the *energeian planēs* will be, it will not be a by-product of some previous action. The finite and transitive verb πέμπει (*pempei*, "sends") underscores the fact that the deluding influence is, in fact, sent; it will not merely result from an outworking of related events.[16] Accordingly, Alford warns against reducing the significance of the term, stating it "must not for a moment be understood of *permissiveness* only on God's part—He is the judicial sender and doer."[17] He further notes that many versions have "weakened, indeed almost stultified the sentence by rendering . . . (it) 'a strong delusion,' i.e., the passive state resulting, instead of the active cause."[18] Lünemann concurs, noting that it is "not a statement of the consequence [for sin leading on to sin], but of the *design* of God Himself."[19] Marshall summarily advises, "Various commentaries have rightly warned against any attempt to weaken the force of Paul's statement, no matter how unwelcome it may be to modern readers."[20]

Still much debate on defining this term, and especially how it relates to God, remains. Usually the suggested definitions are quite broad since the particulars of this verse are difficult to ascertain. Some describe the deluding influence as a "powerful working of error" whose sending is attributed to God.[21] One view presents God as subjecting the unbelievers

---

[16] In reference to 2 Thess. 2:11, Aus states, "God is the subject; he does the deluding, although it is based on the individual's rejection of the gospel. The theocentric significance of this summary statement should not be overlooked because of the more interesting details of the whole paragraph, 2:1-13" (Roger D. Aus, "God's Plan and God's Power: Isaiah 66 and the Restraining Factors of 2 Thessalonians 2:6-7," *Journal of Biblical Literature* 96 [1977]: 500). However, whether God deludes or deceives will be discussed below.

[17] Henry Alford, *The Greek Testament* (London: Longmans, Green, Co., 1903; reprint, Chicago: Moody, 1958), 3:292.

[18] Ibid.

[19] Gottleib Lünemann, "Critical and Exegetical Handbook of the Epistles of St. Paul to the Thessalonians," in *Meyer's Commentary on the New Testament*, ed. H. A. Meyer (Edinburgh: T. & T. Clark, 1884; reprint, Winona Lake, Ind.: Alpha, 1980), 8:222.

[20] I. Howard Marshall, "1 and 2 Thessalonians," in *The New Century Bible Commentary* (Grand Rapids: Eerdmans, 1983), 204.

[21] Charles C. Ryrie, *First and Second Thessalonians* (Chicago: Moody, 1959), 114. Similar wording appears in Robertson, *Word Pictures in the New Testament* 4:53-54; Leon Morris, *The First and Second Epistles to the Thessalonians*, New International Commentary on the New Testament, ed. F. F. Bruce (Grand Rapids: Eerdmans, 1959), 233.

of the Tribulation to the powerful delusion that comes from their choosing error over truth.²²

Other views highlight the element of power normally associated elsewhere with *energeia*.²³ Along with the etymological considerations of the word, a major reason the power aspect is often highlighted is Paul's previous use of *energeia* in the context of 2 Thessalonians 2. Since Paul's emphasis was on the active, powerful activity of Satan (ἐνέργειαν τοῦ Σατανᾶ. *energeian tou Satana*) through his earthly agent (2:9), then an active, powerful activity should be expected as well in the deluding influence that will originate from God (v. 11). Accordingly, the *energeian planēs* sent by God is defined variously as "the power that leads to deception,"²⁴ or as the working of error that could be best rendered "an active power of misleading."²⁵ An even more challenging interpretation asserts that God Himself "leads unbelievers into error."²⁶ Morris agrees, noting that throughout Scripture *energeia* always "denotes power in action," so that the reference to God sending a deluding influence in 2 Thess. 2:11 likewise "indicates not merely a passive acquiescence in wrong-doing, but an active forwarding of evil."²⁷ Gottleib Lünemann accordingly translates the term as an "active power of seduction."²⁸

---

²² Thomas L. Constable, "Second Thessalonians," in *The Bible Knowledge Commentary, New Testament*, eds. John F. Walvoord and Roy B. Zuck (Wheaton, Ill.: Victor, 1981), 720. Though it is true the choosing of error over the truth will be the basis for God's judgment, this interpretation associates the sending of the ἐνεργείαν πλάνης with the normal outworking of God's judgment, such as in Rom 1:18-25. Whether this is a legitimate association will be addressed below.

²³ Specifics of the word ἐνέργεια will be addressed later in this article.

²⁴ Charles A. Wanamaker, *The Epistles to the Thessalonians: A Commentary on the Greek Text*, New International Greek Testament Commentary (Grand Rapids: Eerdmans, 1990), 262-63.

²⁵ Marvin R. Vincent, *Word Pictures in the New Testament* (New York: Charles Scribner's Sons; 1887; reprint, Grand Rapids: Eerdmans, 1985), 3:66-67.

²⁶ Paul Ellingworth and Eugene A. Nida, *A Translator's Handbook on Paul's Letters to the Thessalonians*, Helps for Translators Series (London, New York, Stuttgart: United Bible Societies, 1976), 178. Herein will be one of the main considerations in determining the meaning of the ἐνεργείαν πλάνης: Does God lead the unbelievers into sin? Ellingworth and Nida go even further by concluding that a possible translation is, "God causes them to act very wrongly" (ibid., 179). This point will be discussed below.

²⁷ Morris, *The First and Second Epistles to the Thessalonians*, 134.

²⁸ Lünemann, "First and Second Thessalonians," 222.

Another line of reasoning places more emphasis on the inward effect the *energeian planēs* will have on others. Consequently, God will remove from the unregenerate of the Tribulation "their power of discerning the true from the false."[29] Eadie likewise defines the term as "an in working error" so that *"indifference to the truth* gets its divine recompense in its facile seduction into gross and grosser errors."[30] However, the use of an aorist indicative in 2:10 in describing the deceived as those "who would not receive the love of the truth so as to be saved" points more to blatant rejection of the truth, not indifference to it. Likewise, the adamant refusal of the unredeemed to believe the truth, coupled with their active taking pleasure in wickedness in 2:12, argues against indifference to the truth as the basic problem.

A few factors should be in the forefront in characterizing the future deluding influence. Initially, for God to send some element of deception is not exactly equivalent to God actively deceiving. He sends someone or something which deceives; He Himself is not named as the deceiver. Second, the uniqueness of the future period must be emphasized. The Tribulation will be an unprecedented period of God's judgment on earth with many unique events.[31] Consequently, establishing a precise definition for the deluding influence by either historical or present analogies may not be possible, since no historical situation is directly comparable.[32] The wise course is to deal with specifics of the text instead of attempting to explain it by current analogies. Though some biblical accounts may be similar, no previous account will match perfectly. Another factor to consider is the judicial nature of God's sending of the *energeian planēs*, something clearly attested in 2 Thess. 2:12 as developed below. Finally, the claim by some that God leads unbelievers

---

[29] A. J. Mason, "The Epistles to the Thessalonians," in *Ellicott's Commentary on the Whole Bible*, ed. Charles John Ellicott (Grand Rapids: Zondervan, n.d.), 8:158.

[30] John Eadie, *Commentary on the Greek Text of the Epistles of Paul to the Thessalonians* (New York: Macmillan, 1877; reprint, Grand Rapids: Baker, 1979), 287 [emphasis added].

[31] For example, two important elements among several will be the removal of the restrainer (2 Thess. 2:6-7) and the presence of the beast who will exercise the full extent of Satan's power for three and a half years (Rev. 13:1-5).

[32] For instance, trying to define precisely the meaning and nature of the mark of the beast in Rev. 13:16-18 is, at best, conjectural since such a mark has never been given.

into sin,[33] particularly by means of the deluding influence, must be examined, especially in view of the previously stated controversies. It is necessary to consider these and other matters along with other passages associating God with deception.

BIBLICAL EXAMPLES OF GOD'S USE OF DECEPTION AS A MEANS OF JUDGMENT

The Tribulation will be a unique time of intensified satanic deception, as well as the time of God's sending of the deluding influence, but the Bible indicates God has already used deception as a means of judgment against those who reject His truth. Two OT passages—1 Kgs. 22:22 and Ezek. 14:9—specifically present God as using deception for His purpose; a NT passage—Rom. 1:18-32—may also be relevant.

FIRST KINGS 22:22

First Kgs. 22:22 is the initial biblical account that associates God's use of deception to suit His purpose. Here God instructed a spirit who volunteered to be a deceiving spirit among the false prophets of King Ahab, "You are to entice[34] him and also prevail. Go and do so." Wide disagreement exists among scholars concerning the identity of this spirit. Whether the spirit is an angel of God,[35] a demonic being,[36] or Satan

---

[33] Ellingworth and Nida, *A Translator's Handbook on Paul's Letters to the Thessalonians*, 178-79.

[34] The verb פָּתָה, translated "to deceive" or "to entice," appears twenty-seven times in the OT. Among other places, it is used of Delilah's enticing of Samson to learn his riddle (Judg. 14:15-16), of a man seducing a woman (Exod. 22:15), of a warning about being deceived by false gods (Deut. 11:16), and of Jeremiah's complaint that God deceived him (Jer. 20:7-9) (Louis Goldberg, "פָּתָה," in *Theological Wordbook of the Old Testament*, 2:742-43).

[35] Robert B. Chisholm, "Does God Deceive?," *Bibliotheca Sacra* 155 [January-March 1998]: 15-16. An aspect of Chisholm's rationale is that the spirit is among the "host of heaven" (1 Kgs. 22:19), an expression normally associated with the holy angels of God. E.g., Deut. 4:19; 17:3; 2 Kgs. 17:16; 21:3, 5; 23:4-5; 2 Chron. 33:3.

[36] J. A. Thompson, *Second Chronicles*, The New American Commentary, ed. E. Ray Clendenen (Nashville: Broadman and Holman, 1994), 9:286. For a listing of other scholars who hold this position, see Richard L. Mayhue, "False Prophets and Deceiving Spirits," *The Master's Seminary Journal* 4/2 (Fall 1993): 142-43.

himself,[37] is not the primary focus of this article. God's role in commanding the deception to occur is the main point. In this episode God commissioned the spirit, either holy or evil, to deceive, something not normally associated with the God who cannot lie (Heb. 6:18).

Contextual factors in 1 Kings 22 help to understand this occasion when God employed deception to accomplish His purpose. The chapter records the encounter of Micaiah the prophet as he stood against kings Ahab and Jehoshaphat and their collective prophetic corps. The pending issue was Syria's possession of Ramoth Gilead, a town Ahab felt rightly belonged to Israel. Before going into battle to recapture the city, Jehoshaphat requested that an inquiry be made of the LORD (22:5). Ahab gathered approximately four hundred prophets before him,[38] all of whom counseled going into battle, assuring the kings "the Lord [also LORD] will give it into the hand of the king" (22:6, 11-12).

Despite the unanimity of the prophets' decree, Jehoshaphat was not convinced. Instead he asked, "Is there not yet a prophet of the LORD here, that we may inquire of him?" (22:7). Ahab summoned Micaiah, who was asked by the messenger to speak favorably to the king (22:13). Micaiah's response establishes a crucial aspect in understanding the deception that will follow. In 1 Kgs. 22:14 Micaiah declared, "As the LORD lives, what the LORD says to me, that I will speak." When asked by the king concerning the pending attack, Micaiah mockingly responded by mimicking the prophets, telling Ahab to go to battle because the LORD will give victory to the king (22:15). Something in the prophet's demeanor must have reflected his sarcasm. Ahab readily recognized Micaiah's insincerity, issuing a second crucial injunction that dramatically changes the course of the conversation. The king chastened Micaiah, saying, "How many times must I adjure you to speak to me nothing but the truth in the name of the LORD" (22:16). Thus, the core

---

[37] Mayhue offers eight supports that Satan is the deceiving spirit of 1 Kings 22, one of which is its harmony with God sending the deluding influence in 2 Thess. 2:11-12 (ibid., 146-48). He also presents a listing of various scholars who hold this position (ibid., 147).

[38] First Kgs. 22:12, 24 shows these prophets claimed to be and were considered prophets of the LORD, not prophets of Baal and the Asherah. Further, the false prophet Zedekiah, who struck Micaiah on the face, rebuked the true prophet, asking, "How did the Spirit of the LORD pass from me to speak to you?".

The Lie

issue comes to the forefront: who speaks for God, or, more precisely, what is the truth of God?[39] That two distinct sides existed who both made claim to speaking divine truth is foundational in understanding God's upcoming use of deception. Both sources of "truth" could not be correct; neither could both opposing factions speak for God. One or both were false.

After prophesying that the attack would end in certain defeat and destruction, Micaiah revealed the heretofore unknown spiritual realities beyond the present earthly realm in 1 Kgs. 22:19-23: "Therefore, hear the word of the LORD. I saw the LORD sitting on His throne, and all the host of heaven standing by Him on His right hand and on His left. And the LORD said, 'Who will entice Ahab to go up and fall at Ramoth Gilead?' And one said this while another said that. Then a spirit came forward and stood before the LORD and said, 'I will entice him.' And the LORD said to him, 'How?' And He said, 'I will go out and be a deceiving spirit in the mouth of all his prophets.' Then He said, 'You are to entice him and also prevail. Go and do so.' Now therefore, behold, the LORD has put a deceiving spirit in the mouth of all these your prophets, and the LORD has proclaimed disaster against you." Three times in this account a form of פָּתָה (*pātāh*) is used (22:20-22). That a means of deception will be employed by God is also seen in the twofold use of "deceiving spirit" (רוּחַ שֶׁקֶר, *rûaḥ šeqer*). The verb שָׁקַר (*šāqar*) a close synonym of *pātāh*, is used of breaking a promise or of words or activities which are false because they are without any factual basis.[40]

God's sending of a member from the host of heaven to be a deceiving spirit may surprise some, but other factors are relevant.[41] First, it is difficult to call God a liar or deceiver when He announced *before* Ahab went to battle that a deceiving spirit had been placed in the mouths

---

[39] Chisholm notes that this was the first time "truth" factored in the account and sets the stage for Micaiah's response. "Only when the king insisted on the truth . . . did Micaiah give him an accurate prophecy of how the battle would turn out" ("Does God Deceive?" 14).

[40] Hermann J. Austel, "שׁקר" in *Theological Wordbook of the Old Testament*, eds. R. Laird Harris, Gleason L. Archer, Jr., and Bruce K. Waltke (Chicago: Moody, 1980), 2:957-58.

[41] If the spirit was, in fact, an evil spirit, this poses no theological dilemma. It should be noted that God may send or use evil spirits to accomplish His purpose, such as in the case of the tormenting of Saul (1 Sam. 16:14, 23) and the demons yet to be released from the abyss in Rev. 9:1-12.

of all his prophets and that certain defeat awaited Ahab.[42] Second, God sent a spirit to counsel Ahab to take the wrong course of action Ahab had already decided to take. God did not lure Ahab into sin, nor did God entice him to change his intentions. Simply put, God did not lead Ahab into sin. Ahab had already determined what he intended to do; he was simply looking for religious permission to pursue his own course of action, and even that permission came only because of the request of Jehoshaphat. Nothing—including God's specific revelation whereby He had proclaimed disaster against Ahab (22:23, 28)—would deter him.

A sequential development occurs in the broader context of 1 Kings 22, especially in reference to divine truth. In addition to the revelatory truth of the OT up to that time, God also set forth His truth by means of Elijah (1 Kings 17), and His other true prophets (19:10, 14), including Micaiah (22:13-28). Ahab rejected God's truth and ultimately became responsible for the deaths of the majority of God's prophets (19:10, 14). Ahab replaced God's revealed truth with "another truth" by erecting an altar to and worshiping Baal (16:31-32), making the Asherah (18:19), as well as giving place to the hundreds of false prophets associated with these false gods. The four hundred false prophets also replaced God's truth when they traced their message to the true God of Israel (22:11-12). Ahab did not believe God's revealed truth but instead readily accepted multiple sources of falsehood. Ironically, God then used "other truth" Ahab had chosen as a means of judgment against him. Despite his disguise and precautions, Ahab died in battle, true to the prophetic word of the LORD through the prophet Micaiah (22:29-38).

EZEKIEL 14:9

Another OT passage associates God with deception as a means of judgment. In Ezek. 14:9 God promised, "But if the prophet is prevailed upon[43] to speak a word, it is I, the LORD, who have prevailed upon that prophet, and I will stretch out My hand against him and destroy him from among My people Israel." While particular circumstances differ in this account, the overall framework is virtually identical to that of 1 Kings

---

[42] Paul A. House, *1, 2 Kings*, The New American Commentary, ed. E. Ray Clendenen (Nashville: Broadman and Holman Publishers, 1995), 8:237-38.

[43] As in 1 Kings 22, פָּתָה is used.

22, as are many of the same questions. For instance, if God incited an individual to sin, why would God hold that individual accountable for his wrongdoing?[44]

As with 1 Kings 22, events leading up to this verse are relevant in understanding this second instance of God's use of deception. In the fifth year of King Jehoiachin's exile the word of the LORD came to Ezekiel (Ezek. 1:1-3). This statement is important since the one who spoke for God will again be a major consideration of the pending deception. Ezekiel had repeatedly prophesied that God would judge His people for their rebellion against Him. Many Jews, both in Israel and Babylon, rejected Ezekiel's prophecies. The lack or slowness of God's action became a derisive proverb throughout the land: "The days are long and every vision fails" (12:22). However, the failure was about to change quickly. In 12:23b-25 God instructed Ezekiel to inform the nation, "Thus says the Lord GOD, 'I will make this proverb cease so that they will no longer use it as a proverb in Israel.' But tell them, 'The days draw near as well as the fulfillment of every vision. For there will no longer be any false vision or flattering divination within the house of Israel. For I the LORD shall speak, and whatever the word I speak will be performed. It will no longer be delayed, for in your days, O rebellious house, I shall speak the word and perform it,' declares the Lord GOD."

God not only set forth His truth of pending judgment, He also identified and denounced the false prophets of Israel whom the people foolishly respected and revered. God revealed that such false prophets prophesied from their own inspiration, even though they presented their message as originating with Him (13:2). God renounced them, declaring, "Woe to the foolish prophets who are following their own spirit and have seen nothing" (13:3). Further, "They see falsehood and lying divination who are saying, 'The LORD declares,' when the LORD has not sent them; yet they hope for the fulfillment of their word" (13:6). God declared His open and active opposition against such lying prophets who misled His people (13:8-10a), as He promised certain wrath and destruction against them (13:10b-16). Included in this denunciation were the women who practiced magic and falsely prophesied, thus profaning God's name to

---

[44] Chisholm, "Does God Deceive?," 23.

the people (13:17-19). Consequently, God identified and renounced two tragic effects of false prophets: they "disheartened the righteous with falsehood when I did not cause him grief, but have strengthened the hand of the wicked not to turn from his wicked way and preserve life" (13:22). Contained within this verse is an indication of God's desire for the wicked to repent, but He realized false prophets hindered the rebellious from turning to Him. In keeping with His earlier promise of immediate action, God pronounced judgment on such false prophets (13:23a). The culminating result would be, "Thus you will know that I am the LORD" (13:23b). As in 1 Kings 22, God openly presented His truth as well as exposed the source of falsehood. Anyone who then chose to ignore God's Word and instead replaced it with "another truth," such as the teachings of the false prophets, stood in active, deliberate opposition to God and would receive the just consequences of rebellious actions. Whereas the false prophets may have previously deceived the nation by not being detected (although this is not certain), such an argument could no longer be made after Ezekiel 13. God exposed both the lie and the liars by His truth.

God's enticing or deceiving by means of false prophets in Ezek. 14:9 occurs in this context. Having concluded his previous prophecy, Ezekiel was approached by some of the elders of Israel (14:1). God identified the intentions of their heart by saying, "Son of man, these men have set up their idols in their hearts, and have put right before their faces the stumbling block of their iniquity. Should I be consulted by them at all?" (14:3). Having previously denounced the false prophets and having warned the nation that He opposed them—for one who would nonetheless approach the LORD to inquire by a prophet—God promised, "I the LORD will be brought to give him an answer in the matter in view of the multitude of his idols" (14:4b).[45] God strongly admonished the participants to repent and turn away from their idols (14:6), repeating His warning that He Himself would answer when one seeks inquiry by a

---

[45] Even though in this case the elders sought a word from the true prophet Ezekiel, the intents of their heart indicate that they had by no means severed their relationship with the false prophets. Because of this God would use the occasion of their seeking a word from Him as a means of pronouncing their doom, through either His true prophets (14:7-8) or false prophets (14:9-10).

false prophet (14:7). As with His pronouncement against Ahab long before, God forewarned what the outcome would be: He will set His face against that man and destroy him (14:8a). Just as with His warning in 13:23, God affirmed when such judgment transpired, "So you will know that I am the LORD" (14:8b).

In spite of such specific warnings about the consequences of seeking the counsel of false prophets, some would nonetheless totally disregard God's word. To these God declared, "But if the prophet is prevailed upon ["enticed; deceived"] to speak a word, it is I, the LORD, who have prevailed upon that prophet, and I will stretch out My hand against him and destroy him from among My people Israel" (14:9). Stated in clear and distinct terms, God promised wrathful judgment on both parties: "And they will bear the punishment of their iniquity; as the iniquity of the inquirer is, so the iniquity of the prophet will be" (14:10). Such a pronouncement against both inquirer and false prophet merely expands the pronouncement of God previously made in singling out Ahab for destruction; the core issues are identical. When a false prophet is enticed into compromising with idolaters, the LORD will deceive him as a means of judgment.[46] Instead of light, those who aligned themselves with evil would receive darkness; instead of life they would choose death.

In a pattern analogous to 1 Kings 22, God addressed those who would yet choose to rebel against Him and seek the word of false prophets. As with the prophetic announcement of Ahab's doom, God announced beforehand what would result. No deception occurred in either the identity of those who prophesied falsely or in any question of the outcome for those who, in spite of the strong warnings, would still seek such false prophets. In addition to this, God did not deceive by hiding truth. Neither could it be argued that God led anyone into sin. As was true for Ahab, those of Ezekiel's day who refused God's warning and chose instead to consort with false prophets continued in the inclination of their own sinful heart already established. Such individuals also would seek the false prophet even after being specifically forewarned by God not to do so. Similar to Ahab, what they used to

---

[46] Chisholm, "Does God Deceive?," 25.

replace God's truth would eventually become the instrument of judgment God would use against them. If a false prophet in Ezekiel's day received a word to give an idolater, it would be a deceptive word from God that would destroy both false prophet and idolater.[47] The people were forewarned by God. Their choice lay in whom they would believe, the true or the false, a choice that would result in good or bad consequences.

ROMANS 1:18-32

A third Scripture may contain factors relevant to the deluding influence from God of 2 Thess. 2:11, but it differs from the two OT passages cited. Some see a similar concept of divine judgment in Rom. 1:18-32 with the threefold statement of God giving people over to the course of sin they choose.[48] Though some common elements exist between this and the two previous accounts, other matters do not harmonize. Of particular importance, Romans 1 does not present God as actively sending any means of deception to accomplish His purpose. Instead the text presents the judicial standard according to which God turns over those who devolve from blatant sin into an even deeper bondage of sin.[49] If this text involves deception, it could be more readily attributed to Satan rather than God (2 Cor. 4:3-4). Another notable difference in Romans 1 versus the Kings and Ezekiel accounts is that it exposes no hidden spiritual agents, such as false prophets who present themselves as speaking divine truth. Such false teachers or false prophets may factor in the spiritual degradation for some of those who fit the description of Rom. 1:18-32, but Paul does not identify them. As previously noted, the Tribulation, on the other hand, will have numerous agents of deception.

---

[47] Charles H. Dyer, "Ezekiel," in *The Bible Knowledge Commentary, Old Testament*, eds. John F. Walvoord and Roy B. Zuck (Wheaton: Ill: Victor, 1983), 1253.

[48] E.g., Constable, "Second Thessalonians," 720.

[49] In the account of God hardening Pharaoh, Chisholm's conclusion harmonizes with that of Romans 1:18-25. When God hardened Pharaoh, "He did not override the human will, but this was not inconsistent with His justice, nor was it a violation of human moral freedom. In Pharaoh's case, Yahweh gave the Egyptian ruler several 'windows of opportunity,' each of which the stubborn king closed. Divine hardening was Yahweh's sovereign response to Pharaoh's arrogant rejection of His authoritative demands" (Robert Chisholm, "Divine Hardening in the Old Testament," *Bibliotheca Sacra*, 153 [October-December 1996]: 434).

The Lie

However, in spite of differences, some core similarities between Romans 1 and the two OT examples can be seen. As with 1 Kings 22 and Ezekiel 14, God's judicious use of one's choice is evident. God sets forth His truth, in this case clearly seen general revelation that a creator exists (Rom. 1:19-20), so that those who view it are without excuse. Several reject God's truth by suppressing it (1:18), and turn instead to futile speculation (1:21). In essence they exchange "the glory of the incorruptible God for an image in the form of corruptible man and of birds and four-footed animals and crawling creatures" (1:23). Because of their previous rejection of God's truth, God intervenes and pronounces His threefold judgment against them.[50] God gives such people over to the lusts of their hearts and impurity (1:24), to degrading passions (1:26), and to a depraved mind to do those things which are not proper (1:28). As with 1 Kings 22 and Ezekiel 14, God does not lead people into sin but instead uses the determined course the unrighteous choose as a means of judgment against them.[51] As with the two previous OT accounts, those referred to in Romans 1 replace God's truth with something else, namely, "they exchanged the truth of God for a lie, and worshiped and served the creature rather than the Creator" (1:25). Such action opens the way for additional sin which, unless repentance occurs, ultimately culminates in God's judgment (1:18; 2:2, 5). In keeping with the two previous accounts, God openly declares His pending judgment for such a course of action.

It has been demonstrated from 1 Kings 22 and Ezekiel 14, and to a limited degree from Romans 1, that under certain circumstances God may use deception to accomplish His judgment. Consistencies between the three accounts emerge. God's use of deception is never capriciously wrought but rather is reserved for those who blatantly turn away from His declared truth and replace it with something or someone they deem truthful. In each case an open rejection of God and rebellion against Him

---

[50] "Therefore" in Romans 1:24, διό instead of, οὖν heightens the logical consequence of the previous actions.

[51] Again similarity to God's dealing with Pharaoh is evident. "Six times Yahweh gave Pharaoh a window of opportunity by issuing a demand and warning, but each time Pharaoh closed it. . . . When he closed these windows, he placed himself in a position to be hardened" (Chisholm, "Divine Hardening in the Old Testament," 428).

occurs after He has revealed His truth. In the two OT examples where God actively employed deception as a means of judgment, God initially exposed and identified the source of falsehood before sending His judgment. He further forewarned of the severe repercussions that would certainly follow for anyone who chooses to align himself or herself with the exposed agents of evil. No charge of deception against God is appropriate. The absence of faith and obedience rather than ignorance or innocence played a substantial part in those who would be deceived. Anyone who chose a course of rebellion had their wrathful doom announced beforehand.

DIVINE JUDGMENT IN TRIBULATIONAL DECEPTION

Divine judgment of the rebellious who spurned God's revealed truth is at the heart of God's deception in 1 Kings and Ezekiel. The same will be true for God's use of deception during the Tribulation. Though Scripture contains many details regarding Satan's activities in the Tribulation, overwhelming scriptural attention focuses upon God's judgment against an unbelieving and rebellious world during that period (e.g., Rev. 3:10). Satan will actually play a key yet secondary role. The wrath inflicted on the world is from neither men nor Satan, except as God uses them as channels to execute His will; the Tribulation is from God.[52] God's active involvement is apparent in such ways as Christ instigating the tribulational judgments through the breaking of the seals of the scroll (Rev. 6:1–8:1). However, unbelievers alive at the time will at first view God as one defeated and impotent—if He exists at all. The unbelieving world at large will see the forces of Satan as having no equals and will worship both Satan and the beast (Rev. 13:3). During this time God will send the *energeian planēs* with the express purpose of judging unbelievers for accepting the lie instead of God's truth (2 Thess. 2:11-12). An examination of relevant factors in 2 Thessalonians 2 and how they resemble or differ from the two OT accounts of God's use of deception will provide clarification.

---

[52] J. Dwight Pentecost, *Things to Come* (Findlay, Ohio: Dunham, 1958; reprint, Grand Rapids: Zondervan, 1964), 236.

The Lie

As was true when God announced beforehand that He would use deception, 2 Thessalonians also exposes what is false by comparing it with what is true. Having warned the Thessalonians that they should not be deceived by false channels of revelation (2:3), Paul exposed falsehood by detailing attributes and activities of the satanic agent yet to appear. Paul described him as "the man of lawlessness" (ὁ ἄνθρωπος τῆς ἀνομίας, *ho anthrōpos tēs anomias*), using a Hebraism to indicate his intrinsic character, not merely his title or name.[53] Lawlessness will be evident in all he does since it will be of his innate nature to live that way. The second description, "the son of destruction" (ὁ υἱὸς τῆς ἀπωλείας, *ho huios tēs apōleias*), is likewise a Hebraism indicating either character, as in "son of peace" (Luke 10:6) and "sons of light" (1 Thess. 5:5), or destiny, as in "son of death" (1 Sam. 20:31).[54] This case refers to destiny, a loss of this person's well-being, not to a cessation of his existence.[55] In the NT *apōleia* is the opposite of salvation, the loss of eternal life and the resultant suffering of eternal perdition and misery.[56] The certain demise of the man of lawlessness surfaces before any of his other characteristics. Regardless of the power or authority he will temporarily display, and despite the unbelieving world's assessment that he has no equal, his demise is a divinely promised certainty.

In 1 Kings 22 and Ezekiel 14, God exposed falsehood by setting forth His truth. He does so in 2 Thessalonians 2 as well, as He does with other passages relevant to the Tribulation. In fact, an unprecedented presentation of God's truth to the entire world will characterize the Tribulation. Matthew 24:14 records Jesus' words: "And this gospel of the kingdom shall be preached in the whole world for a witness to all the

---

[53] James Everett Frame, *The Epistles of St. Paul to the Thessalonians*, International Critical Commentary (Edinburgh: T. & T. Clark, 1912), 257. The term reflects a Hebraism similar to "man of knowledge" (Prov. 24:5) or "man of sorrows" (Isa. 53:3) (C. F. Hogg and W. E. Vine, *The Epistles of Paul the Apostle to the Thessalonians* [Glasgow: Pickering and Inglis, 1929]: 247).

[54] Ibid.

[55] Ibid., 248.

[56] Ernest Best, *A Commentary on the First and Second Epistles to the Thessalonians*, Black's New Testament Commentaries (London: Adams & Charles Black, 1972), 285; Joseph Henry Thayer, *Greek-English Lexicon of the New Testament Being Grimm Wilke's Clovis Noti Testament*, rev. ed. (Grand Rapids: Zondervan, 1962), 71.

nations, and then the end shall come." The ways in which God will proclaim His truth in the Tribulation will be quite numerous, different opinions over chronology notwithstanding. Such means will include the witness of the martyrs of Rev. 6:9, who will be slain "because of the word of God and because of testimony which they had maintained." The 144,000 sealed in Revelation 7 most likely have a great deal to do with the great multitude from all nations, tribes, peoples, and tongues standing before God's throne (7:9). Further, the 1,260-day ministry of the two witnesses of Revelation 11 will be a means of God's setting forth of His truth and exposing the lies of Satan. The global impact of the two is evident in the worldwide celebration at their death (11:9-13). Because of the open witness of God in exposing the lies of Satan, who or what is false may be contrasted with who or what is true. As with the previous biblical examples, people will stand forewarned before God's judgmental use of deception overtakes them.

Second Thessalonians reveals additional characteristics of the coming agent of evil. The participles used to describe him evidence the extreme evil of this man's lawlessness, including his total disregard for any so-called god, especially for the one true God. The base nature of the man of lawlessness will be to oppose any rival by describing him in 2:4 as "the one who opposes" (ὁ ἀντικείμενος, *ho antikeimenos*), taken from the verb ἀντίκειμαι (*antikeimai*), whose literal meaning is "to lie opposite to."[57] Further self-exaltation will characterize him according to the use of ὑπεραιρόμενος (*hyperairomenos*), from the cognate meaning "to lift up above," or "to raise oneself over."[58] In the pinnacle of his rebellion he will seat himself in the temple of God and present himself to the world that he is God.[59] That he would enter the temple of God would be brazen enough; sitting there demonstrates a minimum of respect toward God and a maximum claim to deity.[60]

---

[57] Abbott-Smith, *A Manual Greek Lexicon of the New Testament*, 41.

[58] Thayer, *Greek English Lexicon of the New Testament*, 640.

[59] The present participle ἀποδεικνύντα indicates that he displays himself continually as God, not as a one-time event (D. Edmond Hiebert, *The Thessalonian Epistles* [Chicago: Moody, 1974]: 308).

[60] Best, *A Commentary on the First and Second Epistles to the Thessalonians*, 286.

The Lie

Having alluded to the destiny of the coming one in "the son of destruction," Paul explicitly pronounces his certain doom before his advent by describing him as the one "whom the Lord will slay with the breath of His mouth" (2:8), indicating that merely Christ's spoken word will destroy the Antichrist. In any regard, no extended battle is in view, nor will there be any debate as to the outcome. The mere presence of the Lord will render the man of lawlessness inoperative (*καταργήσει, katargēsei*), bringing his lawlessness, but not him, to an end.[61] Before his demise, however, the man of lawlessness will exercise heretofore unparalleled satanic authority and activity on earth. Paul described the Antichrist as "the one whose coming is in accord with the activity (*energeian*) of Satan" (2 Thess. 2:9), indicating that a major aspect of the Antichrist's attraction will be in the extensive power he will display. Because of such factors, the Antichrist will be tremendously effective in misleading the world into thinking that he is God and has no equals.

Having exposed what is false by means of God's truth, and paralleling Ezekiel 14, Paul next sets forth the predetermined and preannounced fate of those who would still choose to reject God and align themselves instead with the man of lawlessness. Second Thessalonians not only offers significant details about the advent and activities of the Antichrist; it also gives insight into the unbelieving world's reception of him. Before the demise of the Antichrist at the return of Christ, he will enticingly deceive the totality of unredeemed humanity. Paul presents the Antichrist's advent as being in accord with the activity of Satan, explaining that he will come "with all the deception of wickedness" (*ἐν πάσῃ ἀπάτῃ ἀδικίας, en pasē apatē adikias*) (2:10). Herein is the heart or core of tribulational deception, namely, Satan. He is the agent of deception—not God. Milligan notes that with "its union with *ἀπάτη τῆς ἀδικίας* is evidently thought of here as an active, aggressive power which, however, can influence only *τοῖς ἀπολλυμένοις*."[62] Braun sees this satanic deception as uniting all the

---

[61] Robert L. Thomas, "Second Thessalonians," in *The Expositor's Bible Commentary*, ed. Frank E. Gaebelein, vol. 11 (Grand Rapids: Zondervan, 1978), 328.

[62] George Milligan, *St. Paul's Epistles to the Thessalonians* (London: Macmillan, 1908), 104. This harmonizes with the massive tribulational deception Jesus predicted in Matthew 24:24.

motifs previously discussed regarding deception in 2 Thessalonians 2, especially the suprahuman element of the eschatological error.[63] Satan will deceive the world at large so they will gladly accept the claims of Antichrist. Yet unbelievers will be held accountable for allowing themselves to be deceived, as Findlay observes:

> The dupes of Antichrist are treated after their kind; as they would not love truth, they shall not have truth, lies must be their portion. . . . For δέχομαι, implying *welcome*, the opening of the heart to what is offered, cf. I. i. g; ii.13, describing the opposite conduct of the Thessalonian readers.[64]

The activity of the Antichrist will be of such nature that it will be awe-inspiring and humanly unexplainable.[65] However, despite his superior power on a human or satanic level, his promised demise has already been pronounced (2:8). With truth exposing falsehood, the only real issue is whom one will believe. Consequently, those who reject God's truth will perish, as will the one whom they follow (2:10). As in Ezekiel 13–14 and 1 Kings 22, when God demonstrated His mercy by warning those endorsing the lie, the same grace is offered here. Those forewarned could substitute salvation for perishing through accepting the love of the truth (2:10b). However, most will adamantly reject God's grace and forgiveness extended to them, bringing divine judgment on themselves as a consequence of their action. Rejection of the truth of God leads to the same damnation promised for the man of lawlessness, as God will hold his followers culpable for the choice they make.

A final element to consider is the substance or heart of their deception. Paul indicates the deluding influence God will send will be for the express purpose "so that they might believe what is false" (2 Thess. 2:11). "What is false" is rather a loose translation. Paul stated the

---

[63] Herbert Braun, "πλανάω," in *Theological Dictionary of the New Testament*, ed. Gerhard Kittel, trans. Geoffrey W. Bromiley, vol. 6 (Grand Rapids: Zondervan, 1968), 250.

[64] George G. Findlay, *The Epistles of Paul the Apostle to the Thessalonians* Cambridge Greek Testament (Cambridge: University Press, 1904), 183.

[65] For arguments that the miracles of the Tribulation by Satan and the two beasts will be, in fact, authentic miracles, see this writer's "Satan's Deceptive Miracles in the Tribulation," *Bibliotheca Sacra* 156:3 (Aug-Sept 1999): 308-24.

unbelieving world at large will accept a specific lie, namely "*the* lie" (τῷ ψεύδει, *tō pseudei*), not lies in general. "The lie" contrasts starkly with 'the truth' of 2:10, which they have previously rejected. Findlay well observes, "τῆς ἀληθείας is not the moral quality, "truth" as sincerity in the person, but the objective reality—'the truth' coming from God in Christ, viz. the Gospel."[66] Especially in its contrast with "the truth," "the lie" of 2 Thess. 2:4 is significant. In that verse the Antichrist is "displaying himself as being God."[67] Again, Findlay's comments are significant:

> ψεύδει the opposite of ἡ ἀλήθεια (v. 10), the truth of God in the Gospel, . . . is here "the lie" par excellence, the last and crowning deception practised by Satan in passing off the Lawless One as God (vv. 4, 9 cf.). This passage, in fact, ascribes to God the delusion that we have hitherto been regarding as the masterpiece of Satan.[68]

Such an interpretation fits the context of 2 Thessalonians 2 since the Antichrist will be the major focus of the deception in the Tribulation. He will present himself to the world that he is God and will require universal worship of himself, deceiving the masses who will willingly acknowledge him.[69]

With these factors in mind, attention turns to the deluding influence of 2 Thess. 2:11. A proper study of the verse can proceed only with an understanding of the preceding context as is evident from καί διὰ τοῦτο

---

[66] Findlay, "The Epistles of Paul the Apostle to the Thessalonians," 183-84. Compare a similar understanding of the term in John 8:32; Rom. 1:18, 25; 2:8; 2 Cor. 4:2; Gal. 5:7; Eph. 4:24; Col. 1:5; 1 Tim. 3:15.

[67] Weinrich states that the vast majority of the Fathers understood that Paul's reference to the temple of God to mean the temple in Jerusalem. Since the temple was destroyed in A.D. 70, they concluded that the Antichrist would rebuild the temple. Accordingly, the Antichrist displaying himself as God is crucial in understanding the deception of the Tribulation (William C. Weinrich, "Antichrist and the Early Church," *Concordia Theological Quarterly* 49 [April-June 1985]:141-42).

[68] Findlay, "The Epistles of Paul the Apostle to the Thessalonians," 185. Findlay's reasoning best suits the emphasis of the context. Failure to specify that *the* lie of the Antichrist is presenting himself as God significantly weakens the deception that will occur during the Tribulation.

[69] For considerations of how the wound of the beast will relate to the worldwide deception predicted for the Tribulation, see this writer's "Satan's Deceptive Miracles in the Tribulation," 459-68.

(*kai dia touto*, "and for this reason") that introduces the verse. The setting forth of the truth of God, the exposure of the wickedness at its very core, and then the blatant rejection of God by those who choose the deception instead of the truth leads to God's sending the *energeian planēs*. In harmony with 1 Kings 22 and Ezekiel 14, what is deemed as the truth ultimately becomes a means of judgment against the participants. However, this will not be the normal consequences of sin, but rather God's actively sending judgment on those who reject His truth. As was true with Ahab and as with those who would inquire of a false prophet in Ezekiel's day, God will lead no one into sin. Instead He will employ the agents of sin, whom the unredeemed have already welcomed, as agents of judgment and destruction against them. After the unregenerate choose the lie over the truth, God will respond by sending the *energeian planēs* so that they will believe the lie they have already chosen even more. Perhaps this harmonizes with the angel's pronouncement of doom on those who will worship the beast and receive the mark of his name (Rev. 14:9-11). One who receives the mark of the beast will have already chosen his course and have his judgment declared beforehand by God. The same will be so for those affected by the deluding influence. From this point onward they will have no hope of repentance and salvation. Just as Rev. 14:9-11 is a pronouncement of doom before the events take place, so is 2 Thess. 2:11. The course of the rebellious is settled, God's bringing it to its previously revealed conclusion being all that remains.

Defining the Energeian Planēs of 2 Thess. 2:11

Obviously, God will send the *energeian planēs* as a means of judgment against the unredeemed, but determining precisely the substance of this expression is difficult, perhaps even impossible, prior to the Tribulation, since history furnishes no analogy. Consequently, approaches to establishing a definition vary. An initial point to consider is the possibility that the *energeian planēs* of 2 Thess. 2:11 may be a person, that is, another way of referring to the man of lawlessness of 2:4. That would then be equivalent to the breaking of the first seal in Rev. 6:1-2, and would harmonize with the sending required in 2 Thess. 2:11. God, through Jesus Christ, will break the seal and will send forth the rider on the white horse.[70] Four components support the *energeian planēs* as the Antichrist. First, the judicial nature of this act is clearly seen, since God will send the rider as a means of judgment, as He will do with the remaining seals. Second, the sent rider is specifically linked to the tribulational deception of 2 Thess. 2:10. Third, that the man of lawlessness is Satan's agent, not God's, is no insurmountable problem, since to accomplish other purposes God will use satanic beings, such as the demons from the abyss (Rev. 9:1-11). Fourth, although he will be embraced by the unbelieving world at large, the Antichrist will become an agent of judgment against those who rebel against God; both he and his followers will ultimately share the same doom (2 Thess. 2:8, 11-12; Rev. 14:9-11; 19:20-21; 20:10-15).

Other factors, however, are against identifying the *energeian planēs* as a person. Second Thessalonians 2 clearly presents specific individuals in the context: God the Father, Jesus Christ, Satan, the man of lawlessness. To refer to the man of lawlessness in ambiguous terms breaks that mold. Even more to the point, God will send the *energeian planēs* as a result of the world's rejection of His truth and reception of *the* lie (2:4, 11-12). The deluding influence comes *after* the Antichrist's revelation and acceptance by the masses, not simultaneous with his advent. In addition to this, nowhere else in Scripture does *energeia* refer to a person; it is an active, working, operative power, that is, power in action.[71] Such power is always associated with supernatural activities, but nowhere is it a description of the one(s) performing such acts.[72] So

---

[70] For various views concerning the identity of the rider on the white horse, see Robert L. Thomas, *Revelation 1-7*, 418-23. While acknowledging that the Antichrist will be an aspect of the first-seal judgment, chronological factors plus a similarity to the three other horsemen lead Thomas to conclude the rider is a personification of the anti-Christian forces operative during the early part of the Tribulation. "The beast out of the sea (Rev. 13:1-8) will be part of this movement and on his way to the top, but at the time represented by the first seal, he will not have risen to be the preeminent one of the movement. At the very beginning of the period . . . he will be one of many impostors who constitute this antichristian force of which this first rider is an emblem" (ibid., 422).

[71] Abbott-Smith, *A Manual Greek Lexicon of the New Testament*, 153; Thomas, "Second Thessalonians," 326; Milligan, *St. Paul's Epistles to the Thessalonians*, 104.

[72] Thomas, "Second Thessalonians," 326.

while *energeia* may be a component of Antichrist's deceptive works, it is not synonymous with him. Finally, that *energeian planēs* cannot refer to a person is evident when Paul describes the man of lawlessness in 2 Thess. 2:9 as coming "in accord with the activity of Satan" (*energeian tou Satana*). Paul employed the same word to describe what God sends in 2:11. A person is not in view in 2:9; no hermeneutical grounds give reason to switch to a person two verses later.

Since the phrase does not refer to an individual, one must seek indications of what it is. A few factors help. First, since the *energeian planēs* is yet to be sent by God, no viable analogy exists. The principles from 1 Kings 22 and Ezekiel 14, or to a lesser degree, Romans 1, are available, but not a historical precedent. The *energeian planēs* will be more extensive in content and scope than the deception in the two OT accounts, and substantially more effective. The removal of the Spirit's restraining ministry *before* the occurrence of the *energeian planēs* (2 Thess. 2:6-7) increases the unlikelihood of fully defining this unique act of God before the Tribulation.[73] The *energeian planēs* will be different from God's previous works.

Energeian occurs only eight times in Scripture, all eight in Paul's epistles. Every instance but one refers in some way to the active, supernatural working of God.[74] For instance, it refers to the efficacious power of God by which He raised Jesus Christ from the dead (Eph. 1:19; Col. 2:12), the exertion of Christ's power to subject all things to Himself (Phil. 3:21), the equipping of the apostles for their office (Eph. 3:7; Col. 1:29), and to the divinely ordained working of each part of the body of Christ (Eph. 4:16).[75] The only other uses of *energeia* refer to the man of lawlessness coming with "activity of Satan" (*energeian tou Satana*) (2 Thess. 2:9) and the *energeian planēs* sent by God (2:11). In each case, supernatural activity is present, and in each case, except 2 Thess. 2:9,

---

[73] For the relationship between the restrainer of Second Thessalonians 2:6-7 and the deluding influence, see this writer's "The Theme of Deception During the Tribulation," 86-94.

[74] Han-Christopher Hahn, "Work, Do, Accomplish [ἐργάζομαι]," in *The New International Dictionary of New Testament Theology*, ed. Colin Brown, trans. G. H. Boobyer et al. (Grand Rapids: Zondervan, 1978), 3:1152.

[75] Ibid.

reference is made to God's divine working.⁷⁶ In keeping with other biblical uses of *energeia*, the *energeian planēs* of the Tribulation must likewise be supernatural and not merely have the appearance of the supernatural.⁷⁷

The *energeia* sent by God will be one which will magnify the deception of the Tribulation. The genitive *planēs* is objective and could be translated, "a working that enhances and develops error" or "a working that energizes deception," as evidenced in the εἰς τό (*eis to*) clause which follows (εἰς τό πιστεῦσαι αὐτοὺς τῷ ψεύδει, *eis to pisteusai autous tō pseudei*, "that they might believe what is false").⁷⁸ God will work actively to enhance the lie of the Antichrist to its fullest measure to make it irresistible to rebellious humanity.⁷⁹ The lie which unbelievers will welcome will become one that they cannot help but believe; they will be unable to resist obeying the Antichrist to whom they have previously committed themselves.⁸⁰ Once more, this is not a matter of God deceiving but rather of God using the lie the followers of the Antichrist have already chosen. Second Thessalonians 2:11 seems to say that the satanic deception of the unbelieving world would be impossible unless God actively sends the *energeian planēs*. God Himself will not deceive, but He will send an energized work that will allow deception to manifest itself to its fullest capacity.

In light of those considerations, the *energeian planēs* sent by God appears to be God's creating the environment by which evil can manifest itself to its fullest capacity, allowing satanic power and works of such magnitude as not previously permitted by God. The *energeian planēs*

---

⁷⁶ Hahn notes the proximity of the two terms used of both Satan and God in 2 Thessalonians and their similarity indicates Satan is also ultimately subject to God even in this exercise of power (ibid.).

⁷⁷ Thomas, "Second Thessalonians," 326, 328.

⁷⁸ Ibid.

⁷⁹ Ibid.

⁸⁰ Revelation 17:17 is a similar concept of God working in the unredeemed to accomplish His purpose. The ten horns and the beast who will devour the harlot accomplish the intended will of God: "For He has put it in their hearts to execute His purpose . . . until the words of God should be fulfilled." The ἐνέργειαν πλάνης will be beyond this divine work, differing particularly in the outer manifestation of activity, instead of the internal workings of the heart.

may be similar to God expanding Satan's realm of operation under Job, but with an intensified form beyond this because of factors related to the word *energeia* and the impossibility of survival unless God limits its duration (Matt. 24:21-22). An aspect of this expansion of satanic operation may be the cessation of the Spirit's restraining work, but 2 Thess. 2:11 requires an active sending of something by God; the *energeian planēs* will not be an indirect consequence of another act of God. The man of lawlessness will support his claims of deity with miraculous works and with the full activity of Satan, creating the delusion that he is God. Not only will God not hinder or limit his earthly realm of operation, but He will also "energize" the deception so as to extend it beyond any human explanation and cause the entire world to marvel. The *energeian planēs* will confer judgment on those who do not believe the truth, but take pleasure in wickedness, and the wickedness in which they will take pleasure will ultimately become an avenue of their judgment.

SUMMARY AND CONCLUSION

God's sending of the *energeian planēs* in 2 Thess. 2:11 is a major aspect of tribulational judgment to come upon the unredeemed. Though unique to the Tribulation and unparallelled to any of God's previous work, the framework of the deluding influence is virtually identical with two occasions when God used deception to accomplish His will. In 1 Kings 22 and Ezekiel 14, God employed deception as a means of judgment. However, before judgment He openly presented His truth to the people, even announcing beforehand what would transpire. Second Thessalonians 2:10 demonstrates the same as true during the Tribulation. The recipients of the *energeian planēs* will know at least the content of the Gospel. Lack of access to God's truth will play no role in their judgment. Similar to God's warning in 1 Kings 22 and Ezekiel 14, God shows His grace in exposing the lies by means of truth, long before the advent of the man of lawlessness. God also establishes a means by which one may avoid the worldwide deception.

The Lie

A second similarity to 1 Kings 22 and Ezekiel 14 is God's sending of the deluding influence to those who will have already committed to rejecting God and following "another truth," a "truth" identified as satanic falsehoods. Second Thessalonians 2:10 states that such people will perish because they did "not receive the love of the truth to be saved." Lack of warning plays no part in their sinful reception of the man of lawlessness. Their volitional decision is further seen in that they will not believe the truth but instead will take pleasure in wickedness, that is, the specific wickedness associated with the lie of 2:4. In addition to this, the recipients of the *energeian planēs* will refuse to believe the truth (2 Thess. 2:10b), which again shows they will understand to a degree what comprises the truth. Consequently, their status can best be described as "those who perish" (2:10a) even though the culmination of their judgment is still future.

Another similarity in these accounts is merely a logical step in the process. With God's truth available and having summarily been rejected, "another truth" must take its place. As with the other accounts, God will use what (or who) the people will choose as a means of judgment against them. God will send the deluding influence with the express purpose "that they may believe the lie," the very embodiment of the lie they have chosen to replace the truth of God. As in 1 Kings 22, Ezekiel 14, and Romans 1, God will not lead such people into sin. They will reject God's truth and pursue the agents of sin. They will receive, worship, take pleasure in the lie, the one who sits in the temple of God, displaying himself as God (2:4). They also will worship the dragon who gives his authority to the beast (Rev. 13:4). The judgmental goal of God's sending the *energeian planēs* is clearly stated: "in order that they all may be judged who did not believe the truth, but took pleasure in wickedness" (2 Thess. 2:12). In Ezek. 14:9 the prophet and the one who sought after him would share the same fate. The same will be true for those who reject the truth of God and receive the lie of the Tribulation. They will experience not only physical death (2 Thess. 2:8; Rev. 19:20), but ultimately will share eternal torment in the lake of fire (Rev. 19:20; 20:10, 15). As with the OT accounts cited, people of the Tribulation stand forewarned of the deception before it occurs and will be held accountable before God for their own deception.

CHAPTER 4

THE WOUND OF THE BEAST IN THE TRIBULATION

Gregory H. Harris

Perhaps no other item in the Book of Revelation has caused more debate than the wound of the beast and the healing of that wound (Rev. 13:3, 12). One of the primary considerations is whether John intended this to be viewed as a miracle. This event is significant because it will cause the world at large to worship the beast, who is considered by most evangelical commentators to be the Antichrist (vv. 4, 12). Later, when the image of the beast will be erected, worship of it will be required as well (v. 15; cf. 19:20). This statue will be built in honor of "the beast who had the wound of the sword and has come to life" (13:14).

WHO IS THE BEAST WHO WILL RECEIVE A WOUND?

THE NERO REDIVIVUS VIEW
Several views on the identity of the beast have been suggested by expositors. The historical view holds that John and the early church expected an evil Roman Caesar to return to life, with most people identifying this person as Nero. This view is commonly referred to as the

Nero Redivivus ("the revived Nero") theory.[1] Kiddle states, "These words (in Rev. 13:3) allude as plainly as may be to a tradition which had arisen concerning the death of Nero."[2] C. Anderson Scott is even more adamant: "It is one of the points in the interpretation of the Apocalypse on which most modern scholars are agreed, that in this legend of 'Nero redivivus' we are to find the explanation of the 'wounded head' of 13:3."[3] E. F. Scott, Barclay, and Beckwith are of the same opinion.[4] Barclay adds, "This is . . . the Antichrist whom John expected was the resurrected Nero himself."[5] Preston and Hanson hold to the Nero Redivivus view as well, noting that "in our day we have seen millions of civilised [sic] Europeans giving whole-hearted allegiance to the god of the Germans, incarnate in Adolf Hitler, propagated by the Nazi Party; and millions of Japanese living and dying for the god of Japan's destiny, incarnate in the Mikado, and propagated by state Shinto-worship."[6] Swete concludes that the reference is to the same Neronic legend but adds a new twist. Based on the explanation by Victorinus, the earliest of

---

Gregory H. Harris is Assistant Professor of Bible Exposition, Southeastern Baptist Theological College, Wake Forest, North Carolina.

[1] Some who hold this view are H. H. Rowley, *The Relevance of the Apocalyptic* (New York: Harper and Brothers, 1946), 173; William Barclay, *The Revelation of John*, Daily Study Bible (Philadelphia: Westminster, 1960), 2:115-19; and Arthur Pink, *The Antichrist* (Minneapolis: Klock and Klock, 1979), 50-55. For a survey of others holding to the Nero Redivivus theory and its origin, see John M. Lawrence, "Nero Redivivus," *Fides et Historia*, 11 (Fall 1978): 54-66.

[2] Martin Kiddle, *The Revelation of St. John* (London: Hodder and Stoughton, 1963), 244-46.

[3] C. Anderson Scott, *Revelation*, New Century Bible (Edinburgh: Clark, 1902), 57.

[4] E. F. Scott, *The Book of Revelation* (New York: Scribner, 1940), 82-85; Barclay, *The Revelation of John*, 2:115-19; and Isbon T. Beckwith, *The Apocalypse of John* (Grand Rapids: Baker, 1967), 633-36.

[5] Barclay, *The Revelation of John*, 2:119. Barclay also says the second beast is "the organisation [sic] which was set up to propagate Caesar worship, and to enforce it throughout the empire" (ibid., 2:127).

[6] Ronald H. Preston and Anthony T. Hanson, *The Revelation of Saint John the Divine*, Torch Bible Commentaries (London: SCM, 1949), 97. While the analogy of the blind devotion to a dictator is useful, the following facts weigh against this view: (1) The instances cited were not worldwide deceptions, (2) they were not accompanied by the use of the miraculous, and (3) they did not include the accompanying eschatological events predicted in Scripture. It should also be noted that Preston and Hanson are completely silent on references to the wound that was healed and the giving of breath to the image in Revelation 13:3, 15.

the Latin commentators on Revelation, Swete contends that the return of the "wounded head" refers to Domitian's revival of Nero's policy of persecution.[7]

Certain factors explain why so many scholars hold to the Nero Redivivus theory. According to a legend surrounding the death of Nero, it is thought that Nero committed suicide with the help of a freedman. In great jubilation the people thronged the streets of Rome in holiday attire.[8] Not everyone, however, shared the belief in Nero's death. Tacitus wrote that there were many who believed that Nero was still alive and would soon return to destroy his enemies. In this sense he would be healed and brought back to life. Tacitus recorded accounts of pretenders who claimed to be Nero after his death.[9]

A passage in the *Sibylline Oracles* may have added to speculation about Nero. This passage alludes to the return of Nero from the dead somewhere beyond the Euphrates River, where it was thought he was still lurking. "There shall be at the last time about the waning of the moon, a world convulsing war, deceitful in guilefulness. And there shall come from the ends of the earth a matricide fleeing and devising sharp-edged plans. He shall ruin all the earth, and gain all power, and surpass all men in cunning. That for which he perished he shall seize at once. And he shall destroy many men and great tyrants, and shall burn all men as none other ever did."[10]

Others, such as Commodianus,[11] believed that Nero would be raised from the dead in the Tribulation. Still others held that the "resurrected

---

[7] Henry Barclay Swete, *The Apocalypse of St. John* (Grand Rapids: Eerdmans, 1954), 163-64. Frank Stagg notes that Revelation 13 "seems to refer to Domitian as 'Nero' revived; the second beast is religion bowing to the state. This is civil religion" ("Interpreting the Book of Revelation," *Review and Expositor* 72 [Summer 1975]: 340). Yet he does not deal with any of the specific details of Revelation 13.

[8] R. H. Charles, *A Critical and Exegetical Commentary on the Revelation of St. John* (Edinburgh: Clark, 1920), 1:350.

[9] Tacitus, *Histories* 2.8. Suetonius gives the record of one such claimant (*The Lives of the Caesars* 57.1).

[10] *Sibylline Oracles*, in *The Old Testament Pseudepigrapha*, ed. James H. Charlesworth, trans. J. H. Collins (Garden City, NY: Doubleday, 1983), 5:361.

[11] Commodianus, *The Instructions of Commodianus*, 41.

Nero" will be the second beast of Revelation 13, Antichrist's cohort, the false prophet.[12] And others held that the Nero Redivivus refers not to the Antichrist but to his worldwide empire.

In response one should note that the Nero Redivivus theory is just that—a theory. The fact that some early Christians concluded that Revelation 13 must refer to Nero is understandable in view of the dire suffering they endured. But the early church could have been mistaken in making this identification.[13]

Also, the Nero Redivivus theory does not explain the concept of deception which is clearly present in Revelation 13. If Nero were to return from the dead, the Christians would not welcome this event. On the contrary they would no doubt have been totally disheartened at the renewed and intensified persecution that most assuredly awaited them. They would not have been deceived; they would have been overpowered. Also most advocates of the Nero Redivivus view suggest Nero came back to life in the early days of the church, not in the Tribulation era. Thus those proponents tend not to hold a futurist view of the Book of Revelation.

THE NONPERSONAL VIEW
Many hold that the reference to the beast's wound and healing is nonpersonal. Some say they are a spiritualized reference to evil forces that persecuted the early church, despite having received a deadly blow, and that they involve no future relevance.[14] Holding a similar view, Vos says the wound depicts the forces of evil that will increase before Christ's return.[15] "The power of evil will gather force towards the end."[16] Mounce says the recovery from a mortal wound could possibly refer to

---

[12] *The Cambridge Ancient History* (London: Cambridge University Press, 1934), 10:742.

[13] For instance two other examples of inaccurate interpretations by the early church are the expectation of many that the apostle John would remain alive until the return of Jesus (cf. John 21:20-23), and the Thessalonians' erroneous conclusion that they were in the Day of the Lord because of their intense persecution (2 Thess. 2:1-5).

[14] R. G. Currell and E. P. Hurlbut, *The Ruler of the Kings on the Earth* (Phillipsburg, NJ: Presbyterian and Reformed, 1982), 59.

[15] Geerhardus Vos, *The Pauline Eschatology* (Grand Rapids: Baker, 1979), 133-35.

[16] Ibid., 134.

the reestablishment of order under Vespasian.[17] However, he also concludes that "perhaps no historical allusion is intended and the purpose of the figure is to underscore the tremendous vitality of the beast. Though wounded he returns with increased might."[18]

However, how would the increase of evil promote worldwide amazement and the worship of the beast and Satan (Rev. 13:3)? And why would the world come to any conclusion about waging war on impersonal forces (v. 4)?

THE REINCARNATION VIEW

Some writers say the wounded beast refers to a reincarnation of some individual such as Nero, Judas Iscariot,[19] or some unidentified person.[20] (A reincarnation is a different embodiment of a previously existing person. This differs from the Nero Redivivus view in that the latter points to Nero being resurrected from the dead, whereas in the reincarnation view Nero [or some other individual] is represented by a different person as his reincarnation.) However, this approach fails to satisfy the requirements of Scripture. Satan does not need a reincarnated individual to accomplish his work. In tempting Jesus, Satan offered, "I will give You all this domain and its glory; for it has been handed over to me, and I give it to whomever I wish" (Luke 4:6). In keeping with the fact of satanic deception in the Tribulation, a reincarnation would not foster the lie of the beast because the Antichrist will present *himself* as God (2 Thess. 2:4); he will not present himself as a reincarnation of someone else. Also people will marvel because of his appearance of death and then his return to life, not because he will be a reincarnation of a person who lived centuries before.

---

[17] Robert H. Mounce, *The Book of Revelation* (Grand Rapids: Eerdmans, 1977), 253.

[18] Ibid.

[19] Kenneth Wuest, *Prophetic Light in Present Darkness* (Grand Rapids: Eerdmans, 1935), 123; and M. R. DeHaan, *Revelation: Thirty-Five Simple Studies in the Major Themes of Revelation* (Grand Rapids: Zondervan, 1946), 183-84.

[20] William R. Newell, *The Book of Revelation* (Chicago: Moody, 1935), 186-87; and J. A. Seiss, *The Apocalypse* (Grand Rapids: Zondervan, 1962), 325; and Marvin Rosenthal, *The Pre-Wrath Rapture of the Church* (Nashville: Nelson, 1990), 208-9.

THE REVIVED ROMAN EMPIRE VIEW

Another view is that the beast whose wound will be healed is the Roman Empire and its renewed worldwide dominance in the yet-future Tribulation.[21] This view that the healing of the wounded beast refers to the future revival of a worldwide political system finds support in the Book of Daniel. In explaining Nebuchadnezzar's dream Daniel told him, "You are the head of gold" (Dan. 2:38). Then Daniel stated, "And after you there will arise another kingdom inferior to you" (v. 39). Thus the king and his kingdom are used interchangeably. Also, Daniel's vision of the four beasts are "four kings" (7:17), but the fourth beast is said to be a fourth kingdom (v. 23). Since the fourth beast of Daniel 7 is similar to the first beast of Revelation 13, the interchangeability of the individual and his empire may be expected here as well. Thus the wound of death that will be healed may refer to the future revived Roman Empire rather than to the Antichrist.

Walvoord explains it this way: "The wounding of one of the heads seems instead to be a reference to the fact that the Roman Empire as such seemingly died and is now going to be revived. It is significant that one of the heads is wounded to death but that the beast itself is not said to be dead. It is questionable whether Satan has the power to restore life to one who has died, even though his power is great. Far more probable is the explanation that this is the revived Roman Empire in view."[22]

Another support for the view that the healed wound of the beast refers to the revived Roman Empire is the fact that this kingdom must be present when Christ returns to earth (Dan. 2:34-35, 44).[23] The healing of

---

[21] Proponents of this view include L. Sale-Harrison, *The Wonders of the Great Unveiling: The Remarkable Book of the Revelation* (Seattle: Sale-Harrison, 1930), 138-39; Henry Alford, *The Greek Testament,* rev. Everett F. Harrison (Chicago: Moody, 1958), 4:675; J. Dwight Pentecost, *Things to Come* (Grand Rapids: Zondervan, 1958), 335-36; Walvoord, *The Revelation of Jesus Christ,* 245-50; C. I. Scofield, *The New Scofield Reference Bible* (New York: Oxford University Press, 1967), 1364; and Walter Scott, *Exposition of the Revelation of Jesus Christ* (London: Pickering and Inglis, n.d.), 279. This is also the conclusion of Roy L. Aldrich, "Facts and Theories of Prophecy" (Th.D. diss., Dallas Theological Seminary, 1942), 44-47; and Richard Allen Williams, "The Man of Sin in 2 Thessalonians 2:1-12" (Th.D. diss., Dallas Theological Seminary, 1966), 138.

[22] Walvoord, *The Revelation of Jesus Christ,* 199.

[23] For a rebuttal of the amillennial view that the smiting stone refers to Christ's first advent, as well as for support for the future fulfillment of this prophecy, see Walvoord, *Daniel,* 73-76.

the wounded beast, then, represents the return of the final Gentile kingdom to world dominance just before the return of Jesus Christ. In this view the wound that is healed "seems to represent the Roman pagan Empire, which having long been a head of the beast, was crushed and to all appearance exterminated" but will one day be revived, much to the universal amazement of the world.[24]

Many who hold this view believe that the Roman Empire never actually ceased to exist.[25] Scofield comments, "Fragments of the ancient Roman Empire have never ceased to exist as separate kingdoms. It was the imperial form of government which ceased; the head 'wounded to death.' What is written prophetically in v. 3 is the restoration of the imperial form as such, though over a federated empire of ten kingdoms. The head is 'healed,' i.e. restored; there is an emperor again—the beast."[26]

THE ANTICHRIST VIEW
While holding that the Roman Empire will be revived, others say an individual king, the Antichrist, will receive a fatal wound and be healed. His healing and return to life will result in worldwide amazement.[27]

WHAT IS "THE WOUND OF DEATH"?

John referred to the Antichrist's wound as "the wound of death" (Rev. 13:3, 12), and "the wound of the sword" (v. 14). If this wound refers to

---

[24] Alford, *The Greek Testament*, 4:675.

[25] Peters argues that this point is the key to understanding Daniel 2 and Revelation 13 (George N. H. Peters, *The Theocratic Kingdom* [Grand Rapids: Kregel, 1952], 2:643).

[26] Scofield, *The New Scofield Reference Bible*, 1364.

[27] Representatives of this view are Lewis Sperry Chafer, *Satan* (Philadelphia: Sunday School Times, 1922), 106; Jacque Glenford Schultz, "The Identification of the Beasts of Revelation Thirteen" (Th.M. thesis, Dallas Theological Seminary, 1954); Seiss, *The Apocalypse*, 325-27; Charles C. Ryrie, *Revelation*, Everyman's Bible Commentary (Chicago: Moody, 1968), 83-84; Leon Morris, *The Revelation of St. John*, Tyndale New Testament Commentaries (Grand Rapids: Eerdmans, 1969), 167; Walter K. Price, *The Coming Antichrist* (Chicago: Moody Press, 1974), 153; Robert Govett, *Govett on Revelation* (formerly entitled *The Apocalypse: Expounded by Scripture*; London: n.p., 1861; reprint, Miami Springs, FL: Conley & Schoettle, 1981), 3:119; and Robert L. Thomas, *Revelation 8-22: An Exegetical Commentary* (Chicago: Moody, 1995), 148-85.

the Roman Empire, then what was the wound, when was it administered, and by whom? Proponents of this view usually argue that Rome never was ultimately defeated by stronger outside forces but instead fell from a collapse from within.[28] Yet, "the wound of death" and "the wound of the sword" seem to indicate that some particular event is in view, especially since it is mentioned three times in Revelation 13.[29]

Another item to consider is whether the fatal wound of Revelation 13:3 and 12 refers to an actual death or merely a wound up to the point of death. Walvoord suggests the latter: "Another plausible explanation is that the final world ruler receives a wound which normally would be fatal but is miraculously healed by Satan. While the resurrection of a dead person seems to be beyond Satan's power, the healing of a wound would be possible for Satan, and this may be the explanation. The important point is that the final world ruler comes into power obviously supported by a supernatural and miraculous deliverance by Satan himself."[30]

In support of the view that this wound was fatal is the fact that identical language is used of Christ's death and resurrection. Revelation 5:6 describes the Lamb "as if slain [ὡς ἐσφαγμένον]," the same words used of the wound received by the beast (ὡς ἐσφαγμένην, 13:3). Because of this close similarity Ryrie concludes, "If Christ died actually, then it appears that this ruler will also actually die. But his wound would be healed, which can only mean restoration to life."[31] Morris puts it this way:

---

[28] Walvoord, *The Revelation of Jesus Christ*, 198-99; and Scofield, *The New Scofield Reference Bible*, 1364.

[29] The word πληγή often means a wound or bruise as the result of a blow, with secular Greek employing this term to describe fatal wounds (Walter Bauer, William F. Arndt, and F. Wilbur Gingrich, *A Greek-English Lexicon of the New Testament and Other Early Christian Literature*, 2d ed., rev. F. Wilbur Gingrich and Frederick W. Danker [Chicago: University of Chicago Press, 1979], 668).

[30] John F. Walvoord, "Revelation," in *The Bible Knowledge Commentary, New Testament*, ed. John F. Walvoord and Roy B. Zuck (Wheaton, IL: Victor, 1983), 961. "The supernatural survival and revival of both the world ruler and his empire will impress the world as being supernatural and will lead to worship of the beast and Satan" (ibid., 971).

[31] Ryrie, *Revelation*, 83. Seiss also affirms this view: "The expression is so strong, definite, intensified, that nothing can be grammatically made of it than that real death meant to be affirmed. . .

The Lie

John's interest is not in how the wound came to be inflicted but in the fact that a wound which appeared to be mortal was healed. He does not tell us how it was healed. He concentrates his attention on the fact that it was healed. Two points only receive emphasis: the deadliness of the wound (*wounded unto death*, and then *his deadly wound*) and the fact of recovery. The expression rendered "*as if . . . wounded*" . . . was used of the Lamb in 5:6, and as the recovery of the beast is clear there may possibly be the thought of death followed by resurrection. This is one of several places in which the evil one is pictured as parodying Christianity.[32]

If this is the case, the deception this event would bring on the world is easy to understand. This return to life after receiving a mortal wound would be unexplainable by human means and would result in universal deception. It would also answer the rhetorical questions asked by the unbelieving world as recorded in 13:4, "Who is like the beast, and who is able to wage war with him?"[33]

Also the word referring to the beast's return to life is similar to the word used of Christ's return to life. Jesus is the One "who was dead and has come to life [$ἔζησεν$]" (2:8). And the beast will be the one "who had the wound of the sword and has come to life [$ἔζησεν$]" (13:14).[34]

Revelation 17:8, 11 refer to the beast which "was and is not." This may well refer to the wounding of the Antichrist in 13:3, 12, and 14.[35] The words "is not" refer to the physical death of the beast, followed by his ascent from the abyss (17:8), which refers to his return to life (13:14) and is the same as his reappearance as the eighth king of 17:11.[36] The

---

. Similar phraseology is used in this Book with regard to Christ, but all agree that it there means to return to life by resurrection after a real bodily killing" (Seiss, *The Apocalypse*, 325).

[32] Morris, *The Revelation of St. John*, 167.

[33] Govett concludes, "This is a strong way of asserting that he has no equal. Something very extraordinary must be his. It cannot be simply a rise after great depression. There have been many cases like that" (*Govett on Revelation*, 3:128).

[34] J. B. Smith, *A Revelation of Jesus Christ* (Scottdale, PA: Herald, 1961), 206; and Beckwith, *The Apocalypse*, 640.

[35] Thomas, *Revelation 8-22: An Exegetical Commentary*, 293.

[36] William Lee, "The Revelation of St. John," in *The Holy Bible* (London: John Murray, 1881), 4:741; and A. T. Robertson, *Word Pictures in the New Testament* (Nashville: Broadman, 1932), 6:431.

twofold reference to the beast going to destruction or perdition (17:8, 11) is the same as his eternal confinement in the lake of fire (19:20). The description of the beast in Revelation 17 likewise contains many similarities to the sword-wounded beast who was healed. "The language is quite similar, the astonishment of the world's inhabitants identical, and the threefold emphasis on this spectacular feature is repeated in both contexts (13:3, 12, 14; 17:8 bis, 11)."[37]

The Book of Revelation uses forms of θαυμάζω, "wonder" or "astonishment," to describe the world's response to the revived beast. The word θαυμάζω speaks of a bewildered amazement, such as Peter marveling on his way home from the empty tomb (Luke 24:12) and the disciples collectively marveling when the resurrected Jesus appeared in their presence (24:41). In the Tribulation the world will be amazed at the beast who "was and is not, and is about to come up out of the abyss and go to destruction. And those who dwell on the earth will wonder [θαυμασθήσονται] . . . when they see the beast, that he was and is not and will come" (17:8; cf. 13:3).

Revelation 19:19-21 offers additional information about the beast. "And I saw the beast and the kings of the earth and their armies, assembled to make war against Him who sat upon the horse, and against His army. And the beast was seized, and with him the false prophet who performed the signs in his presence, by which he deceived those who had received the mark of the beast and those who worshiped his image; these two were thrown alive into the lake of fire which burns with brimstone. And the rest were killed with the sword which came from the mouth of Him who sat upon the horse, and all the birds were filled with their flesh."

This passage gives crucial information not only on the demise of the beast and the false prophet but also on their capacity. These two will be thrown alive into the lake of fire, while the other enemies of Christ are killed, later to be judged at the Great White Throne judgment (20:11-15).

---

[37] Lee, "The Revelation of St. John," 4:789; and Bullinger, *The Apocalypse or The Day of the Lord*," 607.

Thus two individuals are in view, not merely personifications of empires, because no empires will be cast into the lake of fire.[38]

Perhaps the major obstacle in viewing the healing of the wound as belonging to a person is the observation that it is "questionable whether Satan has the power to restore life to one who has died, even though his power is great."[39] However, this is "a theological assumption, not an exegetical observation."[40] Also this does not necessarily mean that Satan is the one who will heal the wound of the beast. Scripture is silent as to the source of the healing. If the healing of the beast does refer to a physical resuscitation, no doubt the forces of Satan will take credit for such a work when it occurs. It is also significant that the image that will be built in response to the beast's recovery from the fatal wound is referred to once more in 19:20. Obviously the healing of the wound is a tremendously important event in the Tribulation, and one of the greatest means by which the world will be deceived.

CONCLUSION

The possibility of the beast's return to life (with either God's sovereign permission or His active working) should not be readily ruled out. In other words it is not impossible that the Antichrist should return to life because of the unique status of the Tribulation and the increased capacity of satanic power during that time, as well as God's broadening the parameters of what He will either permit or accomplish directly. Deception will initially cause the world to marvel after the beast and to worship him and Satan (13:3-4). Deception will further be achieved by the signs the false prophet will perform when he requires mandatory worship of the beast and his image. Such activities will not occur until after the wound is healed and the image is built (vv. 8, 15).

---

[38] Alford, *The Greek Testament*, 4:730. Thomas concludes the same thing, noting that the present participle "alive" (ζῶντες) in Revelation 19:20 indicates that these two must be individuals, not personifications of empires (Robert L. Thomas, "Exegetical Digest of Revelation 15-22" (n.p.: By the author, 1993), 231.

[39] Walvoord, *The Revelation of Jesus Christ*, 199.

[40] Robert L. Thomas, "Exegetical Digest: Revelation 8-14" (n.p.: By the author, 1993), 280.

The Wound Of The Beast In The Tribulation

If the mortal wound and return to life do in fact refer to the Antichrist, then this will be the pinnacle of satanic deception in the Tribulation. It will concur with the Antichrist presenting himself as God (2 Thess. 2:4) and the subsequent marveling and worshiping by the unredeemed world (Rev. 13:3-4, 8). Those who reject the truth of God will be greatly deceived, attributing to Satan and the Antichrist what is rightfully and solely God's.

CHAPTER 5

CAN SATAN RAISE THE DEAD? TOWARD A BIBLICAL VIEW OF THE BEAST'S WOUND

Gregory H. Harris Professor of Bible Exposition

If the beast referred to in Rev. 13:3-4 is an individual, is it God or Satan who raises the beast from the dead? Either answer raises issues to be settled. Some sources leave the issue unresolved, but biblical evidence indicates that God the Father has given His Son power to raise the dead. A third position seeks a compromise between the two positions. The text of Revelation does not resolve this issue directly, but whatever answer one gives has implications for the book's teaching about the beast in Revelation 13 and 17. When Christ returns to judge the lost, the only two humans who will be cast into the lake of fire while living are the two beasts. The two will be the first to inhabit the lake of fire, a punishment that will require special bodies to keep them from being annihilated while there. They will probably receive those supernatual bodies in connection with the resurrection of the first beast in Rev. 13:3, but certainly no later than the action of Rev. 19:20. The beast's ascent from the abyss could not refer to a revival of the Roman Empire, which would not attract worldwide amazement as a resurrected person would. If the beast can survive being in the lake of fire, he surely can survive the abyss, so Rev. 17:18 is probably another reference to his resurrection.

Can Satan Raise The Dead? Toward A Biblical View Of The Beast's Wound

The text has no reference to a resurrection of the beast from the earth, but his relegation to the lake of fire before the Great White Throne judgment implies that he too must die and be raised.

* * * * *

In a recent article on the death and resurrection of the satanic beast, Thomas Ice notes the tension between two diametrically opposed explanations of Rev. 13:3-4.[1] John wrote about the fatal wound of the first beast[2] and his subsequent return to life: "And I saw one of his heads as if it had been slain, and his fatal wound was healed. And the whole earth was amazed and followed after the beast; and they worshiped the dragon, because he gave his authority to the beast; and they worshiped the beast, saying, 'Who is like the beast, and who is able to wage war with him?'"[3] Multiple questions about these verses have arisen through the centuries and continue to arise even among those with a futuristic understanding of the Book of Revelation. Is this actually the death and return to life of a future individual,[4] or is it a reference to the future return and revitalization of the Roman Empire?[5] Furthermore, if Rev.

---

[1] Thomas Ice, "The Death and Resurrection of the Beast: Part I," *Pre-Trib Perspectives*, 8/22 (April 2005): 1, 4.

[2] Since Revelation 13 refers to two beasts, the following discussion will sometimes for clarity's sake refer to the beast from the sea (13:1) as the first beast and the beast from the earth (13:11) as the second beast. The second beast at times is referred to as the false prophet.

[3] Unless otherwise noted, English Scripture quotations are from the New American Standard Bible (1973 ed.).

[4] A sampling of those who understand the return of the first beast from the dead to be an individual include Robert L. Thomas, *Revelation 8–22: An Exegetical Commentary* (Chicago: Moody, 1995), 157-59; Charles C. Ryrie, *The Ryrie Study Bible* (Chicago: Moody, 1978), 1735; John F. MacArthur, author and gen. ed., *The MacArthur Study Bible* (Nashville: Word Bibles, 1997), 2009; J. A. Seiss, *The Apocalypse*, 3 vols. (New York: Charles C. Cook, 1909; reprint in one volume, Grand Rapids: Zondervan, 1957), 321-30. Differences of opinion about the agent of resurrection and whether or not it will be a real event will be discussed below.

[5] Sources who say the first beast's return is a reference to the revival of the Roman Empire are C. I. Scofield, ed., *The Scofield Study Bible* (New York: Oxford University, 1909; reprint as *Oxford NIV Scofield Study Bible*, New York: Oxford University, 1967), 1326-27; Lewis Sperry Chafer *Systematic Theology*, 8 vols. (Dallas: Dallas Theological Seminary, 1948), 4:346-51; John F. Walvoord, *The Revelation of Jesus Christ* (Chicago: Moody, 1966), 199-200; J. Dwight Pentecost, *Things to Come* (n.p.: Dunham, Ohio: 1958; reprint, Grand Rapids: Zondervan, 1964), 334-35; Daniel K. K. Wong, "The Beast From the Sea in Revelation 13," *Bibliotheca Sacra* 160 (July–September 2003): 337-48.

The Lie

13:3-4 does refer to an individual, a core issue is raised: Who brings the first beast back to life, Satan or God? This is a pertinent question since, as will be shown, often the interpretation of who or what comes back to life is based on what Satan can do.

Since the Antichrist will be the pinnacle of Satan's power and deception, some hold that Satan is the one who brings back from the grave the beast from the sea (Rev. 13:1), i.e., the Antichrist. Such is LaHaye's position:

> Verse 3 indicates that the beast, or Antichrist, will be given a deadly wound. . . . Revelation 17:8 indicates that his spirit will go down into the pit of the abyss where it belongs, but he will be resurrected. One must keep in mind that this beast is the Antichrist. In other words, he will try to duplicate everything Jesus Christ has done. . . . Christianity is unique in that we worship a resurrected, living Lord. . . . This power will be all but nullified by the nefarious work of Satan through the resurrection of the Antichrist. As far as I know, this will be the first time that Satan has ever been able to raise the dead. His power and control of man is limited by God, but according to His wise providence He will permit Satan on this one occasion to have the power to raise the dead.[6]

However, if the above statement is true, multiple questions and concerns are raised if John did, in fact, witness a return to life of one who actually died, especially a return to life wrought by Satan. In an attempt to refute this position, Hanegraaff and Brouwer respond to LaHaye's interpretation of Rev. 13:3:

> What is at stake here is nothing less than the deity and resurrection of Christ. In Christian worldview, only God has the power to raise the dead. If Antichrist could "raise [himself] from the dead" and "control the earth and sky," Christianity would lose the basis for believing that Christ's resurrection vindicates His claim to deity. Further, if Satan possesses the creative power of God, this would subvert the post-resurrection appearances of Christ in that Satan could have masqueraded as the resurrected Christ. Moreover, the notion that Satan can perform acts that

---

[6] Tim LaHaye, *Revelation Illustrated and Made Plain*, rev. ed. (Grand Rapids: Zondervan, 1975), 180.

are indistinguishable from genuine miracles suggests a dualistic worldview in which God and Satan are equal powers competing for dominance.[7]

Both positions raise valid points to consider; both have issues of their own to address. Hanegraaff and Brouwer raise legitimate concerns about anyone other than God being the author of life. Jesus affirmed as much, such as in John 5:21: "For just as the Father raises the dead and gives them life, even so the Son also gives life to whom He wishes." Morris comments on the importance of this verse: "The Father (he and no other) raises people from the dead and gives them life. This is the teaching of the Old Testament (Deut. 32:39; 1 Sam. 2:6; 2 Kings 5:7). It would have been accepted without question by Jesus' hearers. There was no matter for marvel in this. What is marvelous is the next assertion, the Son also gives life."[8]

Because of verses such as these, it is certainly valid to question the assumption that Satan could at any time possess and exercise the creative power of God, which is what will be true if Satan brings his dead Antichrist back from the grave.[9] However, to LaHaye's credit, he at least allows the text to speak for itself and seeks to explain the wound of the first beast in harmony with other references in the Book of Revelation, including the worldwide amazement and ultimate worship of the beast and of Satan.[10]

It should be noted, however, that concern about the raising of the first beast as a resurrection of an individual is not restricted to opponents of a futuristic understanding of the Book of Revelation. Numerous

---

[7] Hank Hanegraaff and Sigmund Brouwer, *The Last Disciple* (Wheaton, Ill.: Tyndale, 2004), 394.

[8] Leon Morris, *The Gospel According to John*, New International Commentary on the New Testament, rev. ed. (Grand Rapids: Eerdmans, 1995), 278-79.

[9] Hanegraaff and Brouwer's other concerns such as how this relates to the deity of Christ will be addressed later below.

[10] Ryrie likewise understands Revelation 13:3 as reference to the fatal wounding of the Antichrist since "it is exactly the same phrase used as is used in 5:6 in reference to the death of Christ" (Charles C. Ryrie, *Basic Theology* (Wheaton, Ill.: Victor, 1986), 471. Ryrie does not comment on the source of the resurrection, whether God or Satan. However, in reference to the false prophet giving breath to the image in Rev. 13:15, Ryrie writes, "[T]his could indicate a supernatural miracle (empowered by Satan) which will actually give life to the image" (ibid., 472).

premilliennial stalwarts have also raised many of the same questions and concerns. John Walvoord, who held virtually the same approach to the Book of Revelation as LaHaye, wrestled with the same basic problem if the Antichrist is killed and then Satan brings him back to life: "The wounding of one of the heads seems instead to be a reference to the fact that the Roman Empire as such seemingly died and is now going to be revived. . . . It is questionable whether Satan has the power to restore to life one who has died, even though his power is great."[11]

Pentecost likewise responded against the position of the death and return to life of the future Antichrist with similar concerns. Based on the promise that the dead are brought out of the grave by the voice of the Son of God (John 5:28-29), the first beast's return in Rev. 13:3-4 cannot refer to an individual. "Satan does not have the power to give life. Since Christ alone has the power of the resurrection, Satan could not bring one back to life."[12] To sum up his position, he continues: "Since all the references to this individual present him as a man, not as a supernatural being, it seems impossible to hold that he is a resurrected individual. It would be concluded that the Beast will not be a resurrected individual."[13]

Others have wrestled with the dilemma of attempting to allow the text to speak for itself, while at the same time struggling with the ramifications of what such an interpretation would entail. Usually they conclude that a future resurrection of an individual will transpire, at least in appearance, but leave the means undecided. Seiss is such an example. About the language used in Rev. 13:14 of "the beast who had the wound of the sword and has come to life," he writes,

> The expression is so strong, definite, and intensified, that nothing less can be grammatically made of it than that real death meant to be affirmed. It is further described as a sword-wound, 'the stroke of his death,' or a stroke

---

[11] Walvoord, *The Revelation of Jesus Christ*, 199. Later in reference to the second beast giving breath to the image in Rev. 13:15-17, Walvoord again raises the primary concern: "Expositors usually hold that the extraordinary powers given by Satan to the false prophet do not extend to giving life to that which does not possess life, because this is a prerogative of God alone" (ibid., 208).

[12] Pentecost, *Things to Come*, 335.

[13] Ibid., 335-36.

which carries death to him who experiences it. A man who has undergone physical death is therefore in contemplation. Whether he comes up again in literal bodily resurrection, or only by means of an obsession of some living man, we may not be able to decide. Whatever the mode, it will be in effect the same as a resurrection.[14]

MacArthur likewise, in arguing that the first beast in Revelation 13 is most likely an individual, leaves room for the details to unfold during the Tribulation:

> Whether the death is real or faked (cf. v. 14; 2 Thess. 2:9) is not clear. It may be that the Antichrist is really killed, and God, for His own purposes allows him to be resurrected. More likely, Antichrist's alleged death and resurrection will be a counterfeit of Christ's death and resurrection, staged, as one of the 'lying wonders' perpetrated by the false prophet (13:12-15; 2 Thess. 2:9 NKJV). Antichrist's death will be phony since he never really died.[15]

The purpose of this article is to present a third position, one that is between the two opposing positions. It will address the concerns of those who consider it a biblical impossibility for the Antichrist to die and return to life. It will also offer an alternative proposal and solution for those who hold that the return of the first beast will, in fact, be an authentic death and return to life of the Antichrist performed by Satan, and it will attempt to support this biblically.

PRELIMINARY CONSIDERATIONS

As an initial consideration in addressing the positions, one should note that John wrote what he saw (e.g., Rev. 1:2; 13:3), as he had earlier been instructed by the Lord (Rev. 1:11, 19). Scripture does not disclose who brought the first beast back to life in Revelation 13. God revealed that future event to John, who recorded what God revealed to him, but neither God nor the apostle identified the agent causing the beast's return or its

---

[14] Seiss, *The Apocalypse*, 325.

[15] John MacArthur, *Revelation 12–22*, The MacArthur New Testament Commentary (Chicago: Moody, 2000), 45-46.

significance. John himself may not have understood at the time how the fatal wounding of the beast and his subsequent return to life would transpire, such as when he marveled about the great whore of Rev. 17:6-7. Identification of the agent in the beast's resurrection, if it is identifiable at all, must come from related passages, especially those found within Revelation.

Furthermore, Revelation 13 is not an isolated sequence. Whatever position one takes for the wound of the first beast in Rev. 13:3, will reflect on other matters related to the beast, particularly his ascent out of the abyss, which is actually mentioned before his Revelation 13 advent into the world. That first reference is in 11:7, where the text describes him as "the beast that comes up out of the abyss," who will make war against God's two witnesses. Without additional explanation, the verse simply says the beast will rise from the abyss. More details about the ascent will come in Revelation 13 and 17. The first reference, Rev. 11:7, "gives no time frame for his ascent from the abyss (Lenski, Caird), but later discussion will suggest it coincides with his ascent from the sea in 13:1."[16] Somehow that beast must be in the abyss and ascend out of it, as shown in Rev. 17:8: "The beast that you saw was and is not, and is about to come up out of the abyss and to go to destruction. And those who dwell on the earth will wonder, whose name has not been written in the book of life from the foundation of the world, when they see the beast, that he was and is not and will come." Ultimately, how one interprets these passages relates directly to how one understands the resurrection of the beast in Revelation 13: Do the death of the beast, his descent into the abyss, and subsequent return from it refer to a future individual, or do they refer to the beast as the disappearance and revival of a world empire? Obviously, if the beast (the individual) is never killed, he will never descend into the abyss. Furthermore, if the beast (the individual) never descended into the abyss, he will never emerge from it.

For the sake of brevity, this article accepts the legitimacy of Revelation as canonical, its apostolic authorship, and the many valid reasons for holding the futuristic view of the self-attested and divinely-

---

[16] Thomas, *Revelation 8-22*, 93.

attested prophecy (Rev. 1:3: 22:7, 10, 18-19).[17] It also presumes the future existence of a literal Antichrist and false prophet as human beings who will meet their demise at the return of the Lord rather than as symbols for some supposed system of thought which Christ will ultimately conquer at His return.[18] In that regard, then, most discussion relates principally to those who hold a premillennial understanding of Revelation. Also, since the Antichrist and false prophet are cast into the lake of fire at the Messiah's return (Rev. 19:20), the discussion does not support but presupposes the existence of hell, the Great White Throne judgment of Rev. 20:11-15, and the eternal punishment of the damned.[19]

Further, previous articles have dealt with many arguments against the supernatural nature of signs and wonders repeatedly predicted for the Tribulation. This includes both the return to life of the beast of Revelation 13:3[20] and the authenticity of the satanic miracles during the Tribulation.[21]

---

[17] For an excellent introduction on the Book of Revelation and related matters, see Robert L. Thomas, *Revelation 1–7: An Exegetical Commentary* (Chicago: Moody, 1992), 1-46. Of special relevance for this article are the sections on "Prophetic Style of the Apocalypse," (23-29) and "Hermeneutics for Interpreting the Apocalypse," (29-39). For significant and severe ramifications of attempting to have the book's prophetic events occur in the first century A.D., see Dennis M. Swanson, "International Preterist Association: Reformation or Retrogression?," *The Master's Seminary Journal* 15/1 (Spring 2004): 39-58.

[18] Such as Herman Hoeksema, *Behold He Cometh* (Grand Rapids: Reformed Free, 1969), 634, who about the first beast and false prophet being cast into the lake of fire writes, "There is no question of the fact that they are here represented as very concrete and individual persons. But this does not necessarily indicate that there shall be but one person who is the Antichrist and another individual who is the false prophet. It denotes rather, in the first place, that here we have the end of the deviltry and rebellion and antichristian power. Without any form of trial they are destroyed forever." Actually, the two are not destroyed but cast living into the lake of fire, and are still tormented there one thousand years later in Rev. 20:10. Hoeksema does not explain how a system itself can be tormented in the lake of fire, nor how a system could exist without its adherents who are killed at this time but not thrown into the lake of fire.

[19] The Master's Seminary dedicated the entire issue of its Fall 1998 journal to presentations of the biblical doctrine of hell. It likewise responded to the alarming increase in the rejection of biblical tenets concerning hell by those who consider themselves evangelicals. For articles relevant to this study see Richard L Mayhue, "Hell: Never, Forever, or Just for Awhile?," *TMSJ* 9/2 (Fall 1998): 129-45; Larry D. Pettegrew, "A Kinder, Gentler Theology of Hell?" *TMSJ* 9/2 (Fall 1998): 203-17; Trevor P. Craigen, "Eternal Punishment in John's Revelation," *TMSJ* 9/2 (Fall 1998): 191-201.

[20] See Gregory H. Harris, "The Wound of the Beast in the Tribulation," *Bibliotheca Sacra* 156:4 (October-December 1999): 459-68, for different views concerning the fatal wound of the first

Even though previous studies have dealt with this, one statement should not be lightly set aside as unimportant: the Tribulation will be a unique time in history and unparalleled in satanic evil, power, and worldwide deception.[22] The Bible not only presents repeated statements with specific details about the unprecedented deception that will occur during the period; it also presents multiple strong warnings regarding the coming deception and how to avoid it. The worldwide magnitude and unprecedented nature of the predicted deception must be kept in mind when studying the Tribulation.[23]

THE JUDGMENTS OF GOD'S ENEMIES AT CHRIST'S RETURN

Since the ultimate fate of the first beast is not debated among premillennialists, his death is a useful place to begin in addressing other issues related to him. The return of Jesus Christ to earth begins a series of judgments and blessings that culminate with the Great White Throne judgment, followed by the new heavens and new earth. That the judgments commence at the Lord's return should not be surprising since Jesus had taught that in John 5:22: "[N]ot even the Father judges anyone, but He has given all judgment to the Son" (ἀλλὰ τὴν κρίσιν πᾶσαν δέδωκεν τῷ υἱῷ), the perfect active indicative δέδωκεν indicating the permanency of the Son's right to execute "all judgment." Morris comments on this verse:

---

beast and his return to life.

[21] Gregory H. Harris, "Satan's Deceptive Miracles in the Tribulation," *Bibliotheca Sacra* 156:3 (Aug-Sept 1999): 308-24. Since Hanegraaff and Brouwer particularly questioned the Antichrist's control of the sky and how this would severely undermine the deity of Christ (Hanegraaff and Brouwer, *The Last Disciple*, 394), see within the article fire called down from heaven (314-15) and the giving of breath or spirit (not life) to the image (καὶ ἐδόθη αὐτῷ δοῦναι πνεῦμα τῇ εἰκόνι τοῦ θηρίου, 315-17).

[22] Gregory H. Harris, "Satan's Work as a Deceiver," *Bibliotheca Sacra* 156:2 (April-July 1999): 190–202. For biblical statements about the deception of the Tribulation, see 196-197; for the multiple warnings about tribulational deception, see 198-99.

[23] For a listing of the biblical references regarding the massive extent of the deception of the Tribulation, see ibid., 199-202.

The thought moves on to that of judgment. Arising out of the life-giving activities of the Son comes the thought that the Father does not judge people. This was something new to Jews. They held that the Father was the Judge of all people, and they expected to stand before him at the last day. Jesus tells them now that the Father will exercise his prerogative of judging for the express purpose of ensuring that people give the Son the same honor as they do to himself. . . . This is very close to an assertion of deity.[24]

Later in the same chapter Jesus expanded on the judgment that He will accomplish: "Do not marvel at this; for an hour is coming, in which all who are in the tombs shall hear His voice, and shall come forth; those who did the good deeds to a resurrection of life, those who committed the evil deeds to a resurrection of judgment" (John 5:28-29).

Revelation 19:19-21 describes the first judgment Jesus will perform after His return to earth:

> And I saw the beast and the kings of the earth and their armies, assembled to make war against Him who sat upon the horse, and against His army. And the beast was seized, and with him the false prophet who performed the signs in his presence, by which he deceived those who had received the mark of the beast and those who worshiped his image; these two were thrown alive into the lake of fire which burns with brimstone. And the rest were killed with the sword which came from the mouth of Him who sat upon the horse, and all the birds were filled with their flesh.

Only the first beast and the false prophet receive immediate eternal judgment at Christ's return as they are cast living ($\zeta\tilde{\omega}\nu\tau\varepsilon\varsigma$) into the lake of fire. This is the first biblical occurrence of the expression "lake of fire" as a description of hell. In the OT the Bible teaches that those who die without the Lord await a final judgment of being confined in *Sheol*, which is generally synonymous with the NT use of *Hades*.[25] Walvoord's point is valid and considered standard among premillennialists: "By

---

[24] Morris, *The Gospel According to John*, 279.

[25] Harry Buis, "Hades," in *Zondervan Pictorial Encyclopedia of the Bible*, ed. Merrill C. Tenney (Grand Rapids: Zondervan, 1976), 3:7-8; see also idem, "Sheol," in *Zondervan Pictorial Encyclopedia of the Bible*, 5:395. For a biblical basis of all terms related to the damned, including Tartarus and Gehenna, see Pentecost, *Things To Come*, 555-61.

comparison with other scriptures, it seems that the beast and the false prophet are the first to inhabit the lake of fire,"[26] and "These who were Satan's masterpieces precede Satan himself to this final place of everlasting punishment into which he is cast a thousand years later (20:10)."[27]

The final judgment of Satan occurs later, after one thousand years, at the end of the Millennial Kingdom, and after his final rebellion. Revelation 20:10 states, "And the devil who deceived them was thrown into the lake of fire and brimstone, where the beast and the false prophet are also; and they will be tormented day and night forever and ever." For those who do not incorporate their own theology or philosophical presuppositions and allow the text to speak for itself, Mayhue states the pertinent conclusion as it relates to the eternality of hell: "In Rev. 19:20, the beast and the false prophet are thrown alive into the lake of fire. One thousand years later they are still alive (20:10). The phrase in 20:10, 'tormented day and night forever,' indicates that what their previous tormented experience had been for a millennium would continue throughout eternity."[28] Walvoord concurs:

> In the divine act of judgment which casts Satan into the lake of fire, he joins the beast and the false prophet who preceded him by one thousand years. The text should be understood as teaching that both the beast and the false prophet are still in the lake of fire when Satan joins them, a thousand years after being cast into it. It is most significant that the verb [shall be tormented] is in the third person plural, indication that the verb should be understood as having for its subjects not only Satan but also the beast and the false prophet.[29]

The final judgment depicting all the remaining lost will be the Great White Throne judgment of Rev. 20:11-15:

---

[26] Walvoord, *The Revelation of Jesus Christ*, 280.

[27] Ibid.

[28] Mayhue, "Hell: Forever, Never, or Just Awhile?," 139.

[29] Walvoord, *The Revelation of Jesus Christ*, 304.

And I saw a great white throne and Him who sat upon it, from whose presence earth and heaven fled away, and no place was found for them. And I saw the dead, the great and the small, standing before the throne, and books were opened; and another book was opened, which is the book of life; and the dead were judged from the things which were written in the books, according to their deeds. And the sea gave up the dead which were in it, and death and Hades gave up the dead which were in them; and they were judged, every one of them according to their deeds. And death and Hades were thrown into the lake of fire. This is the second death, the lake of fire. And if anyone's name was not found written in the book of life, he was thrown into the lake of fire.

Here is the final judgment of the eternally damned, as they are thrown into the lake of fire.[30]

Inasmuch as the first resurrection was completed before the thousand year reign began (Rev. 20:5), "the dead" referred to in Revelation 20:11-12 can only be those who were left behind at the out-resurrection [i.e., the resurrection of the righteous] from the dead ones and who constituted those that are raised up unto damnation. The second resurrection, better termed the resurrection of the damnation, includes *all who are raised to eternal condemnation.*[31]

Chafer concluded the same: "*All the wicked dead* are here resurrected and stand before God to be judged. That the Judge is the Lord Jesus Christ Himself is clear from John 5:27, where it states that the Father 'hath given him authority to execute judgment also, because he is the Son of man.'"[32]

---

[30] Hoekema considers this a judgment for both the saved and unsaved alike. "The Scripture future teaches that all human beings who ever lived will have to appear before this final judgment seat" (Anthony A. Hoekema, *The Bible and the Future* [Grand Rapids: Eerdmans, 1979], 257). "If all men are to appear before the judgment seat, this must include all believers" (ibid.). For rebuttal of a view of a single resurrection including both the saved and the lost, see Pentecost, *Things to Come*, 398-407.

[31] Ibid., 398 (emphasis added).

[32] Lewis Sperry Chafer, *Major Bible Themes* (Dallas: Dallas Theological Seminary, 1926, 1953; revised by John F. Walvoord, Grand Rapids: Zondervan, 1974), 367 (emphasis added).

It is also evident that with death and Hades emptied of all their inhabitants, no refuge will remain for the unredeemed to escape their final judgment:

> The intermediate state, personified in the double title "death and Hades," (20:13), releases its grip with the result that the unrighteous dead are raised for their individual accounting. The use of the personification a second time (v. 14) may simply refer to the end of death and the intermediate state, that is, death will meet its end and will not be there to disturb the new heavens and the new earth. Thus, none of the unrighteous dead will escape sentencing.[33]

Walvoord writes of the evident necessity for the unsaved to undergo a transformation of their bodies in order to endure eternal hell, similar to the resurrected bodies the redeemed will have received:

> Like the righteous, they are given bodies which cannot be destroyed. But while the righteous receive bodies that are holy and suited for the presence of God, the wicked dead receive bodies that are indestructible and suited for eternal punishment. They are still wicked and still in rebellion against God. The Scriptures are very clear that if anyone's name is not found in the Book of Life, he will be thrown into the lake of fire.[34]

With no additional details, Jesus had alluded to the body aspect of the final judgment in Matt. 10:28: "And do not fear those who kill the body, but are unable to kill the soul; but rather fear Him who is able to destroy both soul and body in hell." So the Great White Throne judgment concludes the totality of God's judgments against Satan, his angels, and unredeemed mankind.

IMPACT OF REVELATION 19 ON REVELATION 13

As already noted, enduring the lake of fire necessitates bodies fit to endure such punishment vastly beyond present human capabilities. However, in agreement with what has previously been written in

---

[33] Craigen, "Eternal Punishment in John's Revelation," 195.

[34] John F. Walvoord, *The Prophecy Knowledge Handbook* (Wheaton, Ill.: Victor, 1990), 671.

reference to the unsaved receiving bodies fit for eternal damnation, the same thing must be true for the Antichrist and the false prophet. In order for the Antichrist and the false prophet to be two genuine human beings, at some time—either before or at Rev. 19:20—they must likewise receive bodies fit to endure the everlasting torment God has promised. Simply put, at some point the two beasts must change from human to superhuman capacity. This must occur or else the two could never endure the lake of fire for even a fraction of a second, and certainly they would not still be there one thousand years later when Satan is cast into hell, "where the beast and the false prophet are also; and they will be tormented day and night forever and ever" (Rev. 20:10).

The first beast being cast alive into the lake of fire and still being alive when Satan is thrown in makes the restoring to life of the slain beast in Revelation 13 much more plausible. Since the two designated agents of Satan must ultimately receive a supernatural transformation and do so before the transformation of the remainder of the damned, Revelation 13 has the best biblical answer for when this will transpire. Thomas shows the cohesion of these verses:

> It is best to identify this restoration to life with an end-time satanically controlled king who will come to the world as a false Christ. This allows for the interchangeability of the head with the whole beast—i.e., the king with his kingdom—as vv. 12, 14 require. It coincides with further details to come in 17:8 [the beast coming out of the abyss]. It agrees with a final climatic appearance of the beast in history as a person, in concert with the vision's focus on the future (Kiddle). This means a future sequence that will be a close counterfeiting of Christ's death and resurrection. The climax of history will include a healing . . . of an individual that closely approximates the resurrection of Christ from the dead. The question as to whether Satan has the power to restore a dead person to life (Walvoord) requires no answer here. Whether the beast performs this marvelous feat through deception or through power permitted by God, it still brings him into the limelight as never before.[35]

---

[35] Thomas, *Revelation 8–22*, 158-59.

The Lie

In answer to Thomas' question about the extent of Satan's power, this article intends to determine whether God or Satan restores the first beast to life. Attempting to accomplish this may be extremely ambitious, but biblical references give clear indication of whether this is an authentic resurrection or not and of who accomplishes it. Beyond what has already been examined, one very significant deduction warrants consideration: *The Antichrist and the second beast are the only two unsaved individuals who will be permitted by God to bypass the Great White Throne judgment* (Rev. 20:11-15). In keeping with the divine promise that *all* judgment (τὴν κρίσιν πᾶσαν, John 5:22) has been given to the Son, exempting these two from the Great White Throne judgment is solely God's doing—not Satan's. The devil has nothing whatsoever to do with God's judgments other than enduring what God has prepared for him and his angels (Matt. 25:41). Furthermore, Satan will already be in the lake of fire, joining the two previous inhabitants, before the White Throne judgment begins. Since all judgment has been given to the Son, this obviously is the Son's ultimate will and accomplishment. He Himself will seize the Antichrist and the false prophet and cast them into the lake of fire. He Himself has already determined that, unlike the remainder of the unredeemed, the Antichrist and the false prophet—although genuine human beings—will not stand with all lost people before Him in judgment at the Great White Throne. Satan has absolutely no part in this; only God does. Certainly no "dualistic worldview" exists "in which God and Satan are equal powers competing for dominance."[36]

Before being cast into the lake of fire in Rev. 19:20 and before the Millennium, the two beasts must receive *from God* bodies fit for enduring such torment, as will anyone else thrown into the lake of fire. Just as those going to eternal torment must receive resurrected bodies in order to endure,[37] so also must the Antichrist and the false prophet. In fact, these two staunch enemies of God most likely will have received their resurrected bodies before this since no indication is made of any kind of transformation of the two beasts at the Lord's return. Instead of being slain with the remainder of lost humanity and then thrown into the

---

[36] So Hanegraaff and Brouwer, *The Last Disciple*, 394.

[37] Walvoord, *The Prophecy Knowledge Handbook*, 671.

lake of fire, the two will not be killed, but will be thrown living (ζῶντες) into the lake of fire.[38]

That the two beasts must receive supernatural bodies one thousand years before the rest of the lost factors into the interpretation of related verses regarding the first beast. For instance, in part the rationale that the wound of the beast and his return to life cannot be an individual is based on the chronology of judgments in Scripture. In reasoning that a resurrection in Revelation 13 could not be a return to life of a human being, Pentecost asserts, "The wicked are not resurrected until the Great White Throne (Rev. 20:11-15). If a wicked one were resurrected at this point it would set aside God's divinely ordained program of resurrection."[39] But such would by no means disrupt God's chronology. Only a slight altering of the usual chronology of God's judgment among premillennialists is necessary to include the unique judgment of the two beasts, but often the specified judgment of the two beasts in Rev. 19:20 is missing from lists of God's future judgments.[40] Revelation 19:20 is a part of end-time events that is not disclosed earlier in Scripture. Either the Son uniquely judges the Antichrist and the false prophet at His return in Revelation 19, one thousand years before any other humans, or else the two prophetic characters are only symbolic representations of evil systems. Of course, the two beasts will be genuine human beings, as their fate indicates.

---

[38] "Some have supposed a discrepancy between the fate of these two and that of the man of lawlessness in 2 Thess. 2:8 (Beckwith), but harmonization of the two accounts of Christ's return is quite easy. The verb a ἀνελεῖ *(analei,* "destroy") used by Paul does not necessarily mean physical death. It can also refer to relegation to the lake of fire, because the literal force of ἀναιρέω *(anaireo)* is 'I make an end of.' The agent(s) for casting the two to their fiery destiny is unnamed, but presumably it is He with whom they came to do battle" (Thomas, *Revelation, 8-22,* 397).

[39] Pentecost, *Things to Come,* 335.

[40] For instance, though not arguing against the resurrection of the individual beasts in his chart on the judgments of God, Ryrie does not refer to the unique judgment of the Antichrist and the false prophet (Ryrie, *Basic Theology,* 516). Chafer fails to also. In listing the different categories of the final judgments that will occur, including those of Satan and the demons, he makes no reference to the judgment of the Antichrist and false prophet (Lewis Sperry Chafer, *Systematic Theology* [Dallas: Dallas Theological Seminary, 1948], 4:415-18). Likewise, Walvoord in his chart entitled "Major Divine Judgments," omits the judgment of the Antichrist and false prophet (Walvoord, *The Prophecy Knowledge Handbook,* 468). He does this also in his chart entitled "Order of Events of Biblical Prophecy" (ibid., 385).

The fact that they enter into this fate while alive (ζῶντες) [zōntes, "living"] increases the horror of the picture (cf. Num. 16:30; Ps. 55:15) (Swete). This indicates that the warrior-King has captured them alive on the field of battle and sends them off to their eternal destiny in full consciousness and that the two are more than just human, because the rest of the lost will not enter the lake until the judgment of the great white throne (20:12-15).[41]

Probably the best biblical option for the time of this required change from human to a suprahuman is Rev. 13:3, which will have occurred three-and-one-half years earlier than Rev. 19:20.

THE IMPACT OF REVELATION 19:20 ON THE ASCENT OUT OF THE ABYSS

THE FIRST BEAST AN INDIVIDUAL, NOT AN EMPIRE

If the Antichrist and false prophet attain a supernatural status before the events of Rev. 19:20, the ascent of the beast from the abyss in Rev. 17:8 should be reconsidered. This is particularly true since many of the arguments for the beast being an empire instead of a person apply here also. In other words, often the interpretation of Rev. 13:3-4 influences the understanding of 17:8 (and vice versa) as well as the interpretation of Rev. 9:11 and 11:7. Since Revelation 9 contains the first reference to the abyss in Revelation, who or what comes from it affects interpretations in related passages.[42] Specifically, part of the rationale for the empire interpretation regarding the abyss is the inference that no human could ever be in the abyss; that conclusion should be reconsidered. For instance, in proposing that the beast of Rev. 13:3 is the future empire instead of an individual, Pentecost thus supports his interpretation: "Satan is called the 'angel of the bottomless pit' or the 'abyss' in Revelation 9:11, so that Revelation 17:8 does not teach that the head of the empire rose out of the abyss, but rather that the empire itself was

---

[41] Thomas, *Revelation 8–22*, 397.

[42] An extended discussion of the identity of the leader of the demons who come from the abyss is beyond the scope of this article. For different views and their supports, see Thomas, *Revelation 8–22*, 26–38. His conclusion is that Abaddon/Apollyon is not a name for Satan but for another demon.

brought about 'from the abyss' or by Satan."[43] Walvoord agrees: "Only Satan himself actually comes from the abyss. The world government which he promotes is entirely satanic in its power and to this extent is identified with Satan. It is the beast as the world government which is revived."[44] It is further concluded, "[T]he thing that caused the world to wonder was the rise to power of an absolute monarch over the ten kingdom federation who wielded absolute power."[45] This reasoning combines relevant verses from Revelation 9, 13, and 17: The beast's return to life cannot be a resurrection in Revelation 13 because he cannot come from the abyss (17:8), because only Satan can come from the abyss (9:11).

However, the above approach has problems that need to be addressed. Part of its difficulty is in explaining how the totality of the unsaved world during the Tribulation, who will have strongly rejected God's Word as truth, will even know the abyss exists or be cognizant of any activities related to it. Even if the first beast is a reference to the empire, without divine revelation no one would know that the beast descended into the abyss or that he arises from it. Humans will not witness anything related to this; such is a divinely revealed truth. Without the revelatory truth of God, a person has no way to know that this happens. Yet the unsaved of the Tribulation will not only know about the beast coming from the abyss, they will respond in utter amazement after they witness it, as Rev. 17:8 reveals:

> The beast that you saw was and is not, and is about to come up out of the abyss and to go to destruction. And those who dwell on the earth will wonder, whose name has not been written in the book of life from the foundation of the world, when they see the beast, that he was and is not and will come.

Also, since, as noted above, the Antichrist and false prophet will have supernatural bodies no later than Revelation 19, and most likely in Revelation 13, the same could be argued about entering and leaving the

---

[43] Pentecost, *Things to Come*, 335.

[44] Walvoord, *The Revelation of Jesus Christ*, 250.

[45] Pentecost, *Things to Come*, 322.

abyss in Revelation 17. In other words, the text does not require that Satan be the one uniquely linked with the abyss.[46] No human could ever go to the abyss; no human could survive the abyss; no human could escape from there—and yet the beast does just that in Rev. 17:8, as Seiss notes: "Ordinary men do not come from thence. One who hails from that place must be either a dead man brought up again from the dead, or some evil spirit which takes possession of a living man."[47]

The resurrected bodies the Antichrist and the false prophet will have (by no later than 19:20) make them suitable for this. If one can endure the final lake of fire, he can endure the abyss. As before, that is not Satan's doing; God in His sovereignty permits it, ultimately even causing it. Since the beast and the false prophet have to receive a resurrected body at some point to endure the lake of fire, from the information disclosed in Scripture, this is the most feasible option.

RESURRECTION OF THE FALSE PROPHET

Still one important item needs addressing: Rev. 19:20 discloses that "these two [οἱ δύο] were thrown living into the lake of fire." Yet only one beast has the fatal wound in Rev. 13:3 and only one beast comes from the abyss in Rev. 17:7-8:

> And when they have finished their testimony, the beast that comes up out of the abyss will make war with them, and overcome them and kill them. The beast [τὸ θηρίον] that you saw was and is not, and is about to come up out of the abyss and to go to destruction. And those who dwell on the earth will wonder, whose name has not been written in the book of life from the foundation of the world, when they see the beast, that he was and is not and will come.

Connected with this is one final matter that should be considered but is often overlooked. Although not specifically stated in the text,

---

[46] One item that needs to be explored by those who hold that Satan is current sovereign of the abyss is the response of the demons of Luke 8:31. When the legion of demons quaked before Jesus, "they were entreating Him not to command them to depart into the abyss." If Satan were the current master of the abyss, it seems most improbable the demons would be fearful of going there. Besides, if Satan ruled the abyss, he could simply send them back out into another field of endeavor.

[47] Seiss, *The Apocalypse*, 325.

somehow the *other* beast which John saw (ἄλλο θηρίον), the false prophet of Rev. 13:11, must have a supernatural status. Why does the text not say that the beasts (plural) instead of the beast (singular) come out of the abyss? The two, not just one, are thrown living into lake of fire. Thomas muses, "The joining of the false prophet with the beast in this doom is surprising, but not completely unexpected, though, because of his evil sign-working powers."[48]

In attempting to understand this, one should remember that the Bible often presents the spiritual realities behind what takes place on earth. Those on earth, especially those who do not accept the revelation of God, see only the physical events, yet the spiritual side is the real reason that the events occur. One of the examples is the serpent (what Adam and Eve saw) and the serpent of old (the satanic reality behind the serpent) in the Garden Eden, showing both the physical and the spiritual realities. Two others are the events surrounding the birth of John the Baptist and Jesus in Luke 1–2 (the physical births and the supernatural action behind the births), and the earthly opponents (Luke 22:1-2) and the spiritual opponent (Luke 22:3) who lead to Jesus' arrest.

So it is with Revelation 13. Revelation 12–14 is a unique segment within the book. In Revelation 12, God discloses the spiritual realities, totally hidden from the lost world, before the visible events of Revelation 13 occur.

> The method of narration beginning at this point differs from anything previous, because it focuses on the secret maneuvers that lie behind the visible conflict to be portrayed under the seven bowls (Kiddle). That future struggle is merely the outworking of a conflict between God and Satan that has lasted throughout history since Satan's fall.[49]

Before the pinnacle of Satan's man of sin emerges in Revelation 13, God uncovers the spiritual background from which the events will emerge in Revelation 12:

---

[48] Thomas, *Revelation 8–22*, 398.

[49] Ibid., 117.

The Lie

Previously John has predicted the future objectively, but at this point he pauses to focus upon the inner movements that lie behind the conflict that will mark the climax of world history. He points out that the future struggle is merely the climax of a struggle that has gone on throughout earth's history and that what transpires on earth is a mere reflection of the conflict between the forces of God and the forces of Satan.[50]

Chapter 12 reveals the preliminary defeat of Satan as he is cast down from heaven and the woe to the earth that follows in Rev. 12:7-12:

> And there was war in heaven, Michael and his angels waging war with the dragon. And the dragon and his angels waged war, and they were not strong enough, and there was no longer a place found for them in heaven. And the great dragon was thrown down, the serpent of old who is called the devil and Satan, who deceives the whole world; he was thrown down to the earth, and his angels were thrown down with him. And I heard a loud voice in heaven, saying, "Now the salvation, and the power, and the kingdom of our God and the authority of His Christ have come, for the accuser of our brethren has been thrown down, who accuses them before our God day and night. And they overcame him because of the blood of the Lamb and because of the word of their testimony, and they did not love their life even to death. For this reason, rejoice, O heavens and you who dwell in them. Woe to the earth and the sea, because the devil has come down to you, having great wrath, knowing that he has only a short time."

To summarize, Revelation 12 includes (1) Satan being cast down from heaven, (2) the pronouncement of the pending kingdom of Christ, (3) the victory of the overcomers by the blood of the Lamb, (4) the woe to the earth because of Satan's wrath, and (5) Satan's realization that his time is short. By no means will the lost of the Tribulation know about any of these preliminary defeats of Satan, and by no means will the preeminent liar (John 8:44) disclose them to the lost world. The world will see only the physical beings and events before them; they will not ascertain the spiritual realities that precede the events, and especially will

---

[50] Martin Kiddle, *The Revelation of St. John*, Moffatt New Testament Commentary (New York: Harper, 1940), 211-12, cited by Robert L. Thomas, "Exegetical Digest of Revelation 8–14" (n.p.: by the author, 1993), 207.

they not grasp their significance. Simply put, the world at large will marvel at the Antichrist and be amazed by the signs and wonders performed by the false prophet, as the predicted worldwide deception occurs.

That scenario presents a distinct possibility to consider: it may very well be that the false prophet is killed, perhaps at the same time the first beast receives his mortal wound, and that the first beast brings him back to life—that is, again, from the perspective of those on earth who will witness this. God will give the two resurrected bodies, but it will seem to a thoroughly deceived world that the first beast performs this by his own power. Such harmonizes with the uniqueness of the Tribulation as well as the multiple warnings of the deception of that period. Beyond this, it suits Satan's design. Satan does not desire so much world dominion, which he does have to a degree and what the Antichrist will exercise because it will be given to him (Rev. 13:4, 7). Both the beast—and ultimately Satan—desire to be worshiped as God, as seen in the temptation of Jesus (Matt. 4:9), the worship of the beast and the dragon (Rev. 13:4), and the Antichrist's presentation of himself to the world that he alone is God (2 Thess. 2:4).

Those deceived during the Tribulation will respond to the Antichrist in worshipful adoration, as Rev. 13:8 shows: "And all who dwell on the earth will worship him, everyone whose name has not been written from the foundation of the world in the book of life of the Lamb who has been slain." Anyone who persuades the entire unsaved population of the world that he himself is God must support his claims by overwhelmingly convincing means. The Tribulation will be devoid of both atheists and agnostics. Since the Antichrist will present himself as greater than Jesus, he must at the very least equal what the Bible claimed about Jesus. For instance, when John the Baptist questioned Jesus about whether He was the promised one or should they look for another, part of Jesus' answer related to the dead being raised: "Go and report to John what you hear and see: the blind receive sight and the lame walk, the lepers are cleansed and the deaf hear, and the dead are raised up, and the poor have the gospel preached to them" (Matt. 11:4-5). For the Antichrist to present himself as God and be believed in by the collective lost, that he would bring one back to life (as the world views it) would not be unexpected.

Many have noticed that with Satan, the Antichrist, and the false prophet, a satanic trinity emerges:

> It will be observed that the Revelation, in relating the second beast to the first, presents him as subservient to the first. He is called "the false prophet" (Rev. 16:13; 19:20; 20:10), who ministers in connection with the first beast as his prophet or spokesman. We are presented, then, with a Satanic trinity, the unholy trinity, or the trinity of hell: the Dragon, the Beast, and the False Prophet (Rev. 16:13). That place occupied by God in His program is assumed by Satan, that place of Christ is assumed by the first Beast, that ministry of the Holy Spirit is discharged by the False Prophet.[51]

While often noted, members of this satanic trinity should not be taken lightly, nor should their capacities be automatically diminished, especially with the parameters under which they will operate during the last three-and-one-half years before the Lord's return. If the Antichrist is supposedly to be God in the flesh and exalted above Jesus, whom the Bible repeatedly presents as raising the dead, that the Antichrist (again from the world's perspective) will raise the dead at some point should not be unexpected. The healing of the false prophet from the dead would accomplish this. It would also explain the latter's supernatural status that he has in Rev. 19:20. Yet even beyond this, it would answer another question which must be raised: Why are only Satan and the Antichrist worshiped during the Tribulation and not the false prophet? He, too, will have a supernatural body when he is cast living into the lake of fire. That another heals him would also explain why the world will worship the first beast and worship the dragon (Rev. 13:4), but not worship the false prophet. It would also harmonize with the previously noted satanic trinity. One returns from the abyss; and one is returned to life in a supernatural form, giving worldwide witness and credit to the one who raised him from the dead and leading the entire lost world to worship him as God.[52]

---

[51] Pentecost, *Things to Come*, 337.

[52] However, even with this, something still needs to be addressed. A future article will perhaps

All this ultimately originates with God. From the world's understanding, the Antichrist and the dragon accomplish divine acts and are worthy of worship and praise. From the biblical perspective, God alone does the acts and is worthy. In fact, the rise of the Antichrist in Revelation 13 comes only after the preliminary defeat of Satan in Revelation 12. No true dualism exists; only the erroneous perception of dualism by the lost during the Tribulation.

CONCLUSION AND SIGNIFICANCE

The realization that the Antichrist and the false prophet will be judged uniquely and exclusively by the Son in Rev. 19:20 and will be mandated by God to bypass the Great White Throne judgment has far-reaching implications. First, it permits a more natural understanding of the language of the Book of Revelation, something which those who hold to the premillennial reign of Jesus Christ frequently emphasize. Realizing that a change from the human to the supernatural must occur for the Antichrist and the false prophet by this point certainly adds to the possibility that it may be sooner, such as in Rev. 13:3 and 17:8. It further explains the marveling of the unbelieving masses that is predicted for the Tribulation and how they will respond in abject amazement. Since the lost will marvel with abject wonder at the return of the first beast from the abyss, obviously they will not be expecting his return from the dead. Having brazenly rejected the truth of God, when the Antichrist returns from the grave, the deceived of the Tribulation will embrace the lie, "with all the deception of wickedness for those who perish, because they did not receive the love of the truth so as to be saved. And for this reason God will send upon them a deluding influence so that they might believe what is false, in order that they all may be judged who did not believe the truth, but took pleasure in wickedness" (2 Thess. 2:10-12). This underscores the absolute sovereignty of God in all areas, including even a supernatural return from the dead. Even in the pinnacle of Satan's reign on earth, God remains fully in control. Although Satan and the Antichrist

---

consider why the beast from the earth went down to the abyss rather than to Hades, which is where lost humanity goes to await the final judgment.

The Lie

will take credit for it, this will come about only by God's sovereign doing, something, of course, which the deceived world will in no way acknowledge at that time.

Second, premillennialists should amend slightly their theology concerning the final judgments of God, especially in reference to Rev. 20:11-15. All the unredeemed will appear before Jesus at the Great White Throne judgment, all except two, and this by God's sovereign design and disclosure. This by no means undermines a premillennial understanding of God's judgments. It actually strengthens it in that it allows the text to speak for itself, as God has revealed a unique judgment in store for two of His unique opponents.

Thirdly, God being the ultimate source of the first beast's return and of the two resurrected bodies in Revelation 19:20 refutes every criticism and concern that Hanegraaff and Brouwer raise regarding the return to life of the beast. Only God has the power to raise the dead, not Satan. The Antichrist does not raise himself; God raises him. Satan by no means possesses creative power; God alone does, although Satan will lie about this in the future, receiving worship that is not properly due him (Rev. 13:4). So though it will appear to the unbelieving world not so much that God has no equals but rather that Satan has no equals, Scripture plainly indicates that is never so. Satan operates only when God allows and only to the degree God allows. By no means whatsoever could such a view be considered a dualism between God and Satan whereby they exist as competing equals. They are not; they never have been; they never will be, even in the height of the Tribulation and the accompanying predicted deception.

When the unsaved masses respond in bewildered adoration at the return of the beast from death, asking in Rev. 13:4, "Who is like the beast? Who is able to make war with him?" God has already provided the answer in His Word. The One who is able to wage war with the beast is the one whose attributes have already been delineated in detail in Revelation 1–5, in particular in Rev. 1:5 where Jesus is called "the ruler of the kings of the earth," which, of course, includes the Antichrist. Even more so, the one who is able to wage war with the beast is the one to whom *all* judgment is given. He is also the one who declares, "and I have [ἔχω, present active indicative] the keys of death and of Hades" (Rev. 1:18), which, incidentally, is further evidence that the return of the first beast from death is not Satan's doing, but solely God's.

# CHAPTER 6

PREMILLENNIALISM IN THE NEW TESTAMENT: FIVE BIBLICALLY DOCTRINAL TRUTHS

Gregory H. Harris Professor of Bible Exposition
The Master's Seminary

Many scholars hold that premillennial statements are found only in Revelation 20:1–10. Although these verses are extremely important in supporting the premillennial doctrine, many other verses throughout the New Testament also offer support for premillennialism. Our study limits itself to five biblically doctrinal premillennial truths from the New Testament that seamlessly blend throughout the Bible with the person and work—and reign—of Jesus the Messiah on earth after His Second Coming.

* * * * *

INTRODUCTION

Whenever discussions between premillennialists and amillennialists occur, Revelation 19 and 20 is usually the section of Scripture on which many base their argumentation, especially Revelation 20:1–10. Before we examine these specific passages, we know that God has already made several prophecies elsewhere. And how one interprets these passages has been determined long before by how those other related futuristic biblical texts have already been interpreted, before ever approaching certain crucial biblical passages such as Revelation 20:1–10. So, as we shall see, one should actually end the argumentation for this important component of eschatological theology in Revelation 19–20, not start there. In setting forth the New Testament case for premillennialism we will present the following: (1) a presentation of three of the five premillennial biblical truths from the New Testament; (2) a brief examination of two totally different approaches to Revelation 20 among evangelicals; (3) initial considerations of what being in the abyss requires; (4) the biblical definition and requirements for being imprisoned in the abyss; (5) an examination of when did or when will the binding of Satan in the abyss occur; (6) a consideration of two of the different biblical accounts for the actual Triumphal Entry and their significance; and (7) a presentation of the final two of five premillennial doctrinal truths from Revelation 20:1–10.

THREE FOUNDATIONAL BIBLICAL PREMILLENNIAL TRUTHS FROM THE NEW TESTAMENT

Although many additional Scriptural supports could be added, we will limit these to five biblically doctrinal truths from the New Testament supporting premillennialism. Since our first premillennial doctrine comes from Matthew, it is relevant to note the chronological switch and emphasis the author made: "The book of the genealogy of Jesus Christ, the son of David, the son of Abraham." Everything in Matthew's Gospel sets out to prove that Jesus and He alone is the promised Christ/Messiah Whom God sent—and we clearly see this in Matthew 21.[1]

New Testament Premillennial Doctrinal Truth #1: *The real Triumphal Entry has not yet occurred (Matt. 21:1–11) because very*

---

[1] Leon Morris, *The Gospel According to Matthew*, Pillar New Testament Commentary (Grand Rapids: Eerdmans, 1992), 20, writes: [Son of David] "used here shows that Matthew plans to bring out what is meant by the Davidic Messiah. Interestingly, he uses it most frequently when people are appealing to Jesus for help (9:27; 15:22; 20:30–31). But it also appears in the story of the triumphal entry (21:9, 15), indicating that Matthew is not unaware of the royal associations of the term. His book is to be about one who fulfilled all that is meant in being the descendant of Israel's greatest king."

specific promises and prophecies from the Davidic and the Abrahamic Covenants remain—that must be fulfilled—and will not be fulfilled until Jesus' next entry into Jerusalem, which will occur at the real Triumphal Entry.

Matthew 21:1–11 is almost universally—and erroneously—called the Triumphal Entry, but Scripture clearly shows this is not the Messiah's true Triumphal Entry. We must remember that chapter titles and/or subtitles placed in Scripture are human inventions and are not inspired. Some of the chapter headings are much more helpful and factual than others, but Matthew 21 and parallel accounts that subtitle this, "The Triumphal Entry," contain one of the most inaccurate and misleading chapter headings or subtitles in the Bible, and yet this erroneous name has become deeply entrenched in the minds of many people as biblical doctrine. A more accurate subtitle would be "The Lowly Entry of the Messiah Who Will Give His Life for Ransom for Many in the Blood of the New Covenant," as seen in Matthew 21:1–5:

> And when they had approached Jerusalem and had come to Bethphage, to the Mount of Olives, then Jesus sent two disciples, saying to them, "Go into the village opposite you, and immediately you will find a donkey tied there and a colt with her; untie them, and bring them to Me. And if anyone says something to you, you shall say, 'The Lord has need of them,' and immediately he will send them."
> Now this took place that what was spoken through the prophet might be fulfilled, saying,
> "SAY TO THE DAUGHTER OF ZION, 'BEHOLD YOUR KING IS COMING TO YOU, GENTLE AND MOUNTED ON A DONKEY, EVEN ON A COLT, THE FOAL OF A BEAST OF BURDEN.'"

Matthew used a direct quote of Zechariah 9:9 and presented this prophecy as specifically being fulfilled that day when Messiah Jesus, the King of the Jews, humble and gentle, entered Jerusalem:

> Rejoice greatly, O daughter of Zion! Shout in triumph, O daughter of Jerusalem!
> Behold, your king is coming to you; He is just and endowed with salvation, Humble, and mounted on a donkey, even on a colt, the foal of a donkey.

Jesus the Messiah fulfilled even the smallest detail of God's prophecy in Zechariah 9:9 when He rode silently into Jerusalem, including using the two animals that Scripture required that the Messiah used, which we should expect with this fulfillment because Scripture cannot be broken (John 10:35). However, what many people omit in their theology is the next verse, Zechariah 9:10, that continues to disclose divine revelation about God's Messiah, and *nothing* from that verse was fulfilled that day. The prophecies in this verse remain at the present time unfulfilled prophecies that *must* be fulfilled at the true Triumphal Entry of Jesus to Jerusalem. Zechariah 9:10 continues:

> And I will cut off the chariot from Ephraim, and the horse from Jerusalem; and the bow of war will be cut off. And He will speak peace to the nations; and His dominion will be from sea to sea, and from the [Euphrates] River to the ends of the earth.

When the Messiah returns, as part of His activities under the Davidic Covenant requirements, He will break the bow of war and speak peace to the nations, with Jerusalem being the capital of His worldwide rule. And in keeping with the land promises of the Abrahamic Covenant, He will have the Euphrates River as the northern border of the Abrahamic Covenant land promises as part of His worldwide reign. All of Zechariah 9:10 must be exactly fulfilled as was every part of Zechariah 9:9. We should expect God to do no less.[2]

New Testament Premillennial Doctrinal Truth #2: *Christ Jesus did not accept the praise of the collective Jews at what most people call "the Triumphal Entry" (Matt. 21:1–11), but vows to accept these exact praises—and many more—at some undisclosed time in the future from the descendants of these same Jewish people (Matt. 23:37–39), thus*

---

[2] Charles L. Feinberg, *God Remembers: A Study of Zechariah* (Portland, OR: Multnomah Press, 1965), 129, writes: "Having laid the foundation for peace in the blood of His Cross, He now puts into effect peace for all the world. He destroys all instruments of war from His people and by so much from all the nations. Compare Isaiah 9:4–6 for some order or method of peace is given her. No defenses for carnal reliance will be left. All symbols of earthly might and oppression will be brought to naught. This will be done not by the meek Lamb of God, but by the wrath of the Lamb, the Lion roaring out of Zion."

The Lie

making Jesus' next entry into Jerusalem His real Triumphal Entry, at the beginning of His Millennial Kingdom reign.

In describing what is generally accepted as "The Triumphal Entry," the Jewish multitudes shouted out from Psalm 118:25–26 Messianic titles attributed to Jesus, as Matthew 21:8–11 reveals:

> And the disciples went and did just as Jesus had directed them, and brought the donkey and the colt, and laid on them their garments, on which He sat. And most of the multitude spread their garments in the road, and others were cutting branches from the trees, and spreading them in the road.
> And the multitudes going before Him, and those who followed after were crying out, saying,
> "Hosanna to the Son of David; BLESSED IS HE WHO COMES IN THE NAME OF THE LORD; Hosanna in the highest!" [Ps. 118:26]
> And when He had entered Jerusalem, all the city was stirred, saying, "Who is this?" And the multitudes were saying, "This is the prophet Jesus, from Nazareth in Galilee."

After Jesus had cleansed His own Temple and had engaged in various mostly hostile interactions with various religious groups in Matthew 21–22, Jesus began a series of "Woe to you, scribes and Pharisees, hypocrites!" denunciations of the religious leaders (Matt. 23:13–36). At the end of this section of Scripture, in the last public teaching by Jesus before the events leading to His crucifixion, Jesus bemoaned most of national Israel's and Jerusalem's grievous sin of not having believed Him—and received Him—as God's true Messiah. But Jesus also made unbreakable promises to this same Jewish people, as are clearly shown in Matthew 23:37–39:

> "O Jerusalem, Jerusalem, who kills the prophets and stones those who are sent to her! How often I wanted to gather your children together, the way a hen gathers her chicks under her wings, and you were unwilling.
> "Behold, your house is being left to you desolate!
> "For I say to you, from now on you shall not see Me until you say, 'BLESSED IS HE WHO COMES IN THE NAME OF THE LORD!'" [Ps. 118:26]

Jesus made multiple and eternally important declarations that day. First, He told the Jewish people "Behold, your house is being left to you desolate." If Jesus had stopped at that point, the Jewish people would have been in eternal trouble and would not have obtained any hope for their future. Second, Jesus did not tell the Jewish people they (collectively) were finished with Him, because He had not rejected them (collectively) because God's Messiah spoke of His future dealings with this same Jewish people. In fact, instead of totally rejecting the Jews, Jesus told them just the opposite: "You will not see Me *until*," noting the base requirement for them nationally to see Him again, "until you"—Jerusalem and the collective Jewish people, at some undisclosed, God-ordained time in the future—say, "Blessed is He who comes in the name of the LORD"—and this is important—citing from this *same* Psalm 118:26. Jesus did not declare "if you say;" this *must* happen in the future, exactly as Jesus has prophesied. This probably would have been extremely confusing to the original hearers of Jesus' promises. Many who heard Him make this statement had already cried out or had already sung Psalm 118:26 a few days earlier in Matthew 21. Third, the way by which Jesus responded shows that during His earlier entry into Jerusalem (Matt. 21:1–11), He did *not* accept the Jewish people's usage of the Messianic Psalm 118 in reference to Him that day but that He will accept it from the descendants of this same Jewish people at His real Triumphal Entry that occurs only when He returns in glory to reign (Zechariah 14; Matt. 16:27–28; Revelation 19–20). Simply stated, the text clearly shows that Jesus did not totally reject and abandon the Jewish nation. Fourth, we should remember and include God's promise earlier in Ezekiel 20:33: "'As I live', declares the Lord God, 'surely with a mighty hand and with an outstretched arm and with wrath poured out, I shall be king over you.'" The context of Ezekiel 20:33 proves that the "you" referred to are the Jewish people at some time in the future, with Jesus being their King—not just their Savior—at His return to earth and His genuine Triumphal Entry into Jerusalem.

New Testament Premillennial Doctrinal Truth #3: *Scripture repeatedly shows that the Godhead will maintain and save a remnant of the Jewish people, beginning in the Tribulation and leading into the Millennial reign of Jesus.*

This New Testament premillennial truth was presented as part of the Faculty Lecture Series on "Premillennialism," at The Master's Seminary on February 8, 2018, but time did not permit then—nor in this article—the full treatment that this vital component of biblical doctrine could have and should have received. However, even this one simple truth is eternally binding: if all we had from Scripture were Jesus' words and actions in Matthew 21:1–9 and 23:37–39, this would still *require* that a remnant of some generation of Jewish people in the future will be saved by Him as part of the events associated with His return, including the promise of Psalm 118:26 and other such verses given in praise to Jesus by the saved Jewish remnant—*and* Jesus' acceptance this time of both the people and their praise. There is a much longer biblical trail with many more verses that could support this critically important doctrinal truth that occurs so frequently in Scripture.[3]

A BRIEF EXAMINATION OF TWO TOTALLY DIFFERENT APPROACHES TO REVELATION 20

Before going to the final two (of five) premillennial doctrinal truths from the New Testament for this article, Revelation 20:1–3 must be considered because this passage is so important to both interpretative sides:

> And I saw an angel coming down from heaven, having the key of the abyss and a great chain in his hand. And he laid hold of the dragon, the serpent of old, who is the devil and Satan, and bound him for a thousand years, and threw him into the abyss, and shut it and sealed it over him, so that he should not deceive the nations any longer, until the thousand years were completed; after these things he must be released for a short time.

---

[3] See Greg Harris, *The Bible Expositor's Handbook—New Testament Digital Edition* (B & H Academic, 2018), the chapter entitled "And How Shall They Hear Without a Preacher?" for the biblical trail of God's repeated promises to save a Jewish remnant as part of His future Messianic work.

In writing about Revelation 20:1–3, Walvoord does not exaggerate the massive theological divide that emerges from these verses: "The dramatic prophecy contained in these three verses has been the subject of endless dispute because to some extent the whole controversy between premillenarians and amillenarians hangs upon it."[4] Powell considers "Revelation 20:1–6 is perhaps the most controversial passage in the Book of Revelation."[5] Obviously, Revelation 20:1–6, and subsequent verses, are not verses that should be interpreted in a vacuum, isolated and removed from the rest of the Scripture. Consequently, the way one approaches the events from Revelation 19:11–20:10 greatly factors into its interpretation—but even more important—one's approach to this section of the Bible has already been determined in (or by) one's theology and interpretation long before ever coming to the specifics of Revelation 20.

For those who hold to Scripture as being God's Word, Powell presents two distinct groups of interpretation of this prophecy, and the first he calls the "preconsummationist perspective:" "In this view the events of [Revelation 20:] 1–6 will occur *before* the return of Christ to the earth. Most preconsummationists have adopted a recapitulation view of the passage, an approach usually associated with amillennialism including both the amillennial and postmillennial views of Revelation:"[6]

> This preconsummationist-recapitulation-amillennial view includes the following tenets. (1) The binding of Satan represents Christ's victory over the powers of darkness accomplished at the cross. (2) The one thousand years are symbolic of a long, indeterminate period corresponding to the church age. (3) Satan will be loosed briefly to wreak havoc and persecute the church. (4) The fire coming down from heaven to consume the wicked is symbolic of Christ's second coming. (5) A general resurrection and

---

[4] John F. Walvoord, *The Revelation of Jesus Christ* (Chicago: Moody, 1966), 290.

[5] Charles E. Powell, "Progression versus Recapitulation in Revelation 20:1–6," *Bibliotheca Sacra* 163: no. 649 (January-March 2006): 94.

[6] Ibid.

judgment of the wicked and the righteous will occur at Christ's coming, followed by the creation of the new heavens and a new earth.[7]

Sam Storms, in his book *Kingdom Come*, is a representative of this position and presents what he sees as a serious problem against any premillennial interpretation:

> If we were to take the events of 20:1–3 as historically subsequent to the events of 19:11–21, a serious problem arises in that 20:1–3 would describe an action designed to prevent Satanic deception of the nations who had already been *deceived* (16:13–16) and consequently *destroyed* in 19:19–21. In other words, it makes little sense to speak of protecting the nations from deception by Satan in 20:1–3 *after* they have just been both deceived by Satan (16:16; cf 19:19–20) and destroyed by Christ at his return (19:11–21; cf. 19:19–20).[8]

Storms explains Satan's binding in Revelation 20:1–3 thusly: "The Gentiles ('nations') are portrayed as being in darkness with respect to the gospel, having been blinded ('deceived') while under the dominion of Satan. However, as a result of Christ's first coming, such deception no longer obtains. The nations or Gentiles may now receive the forgiveness of sins and the divine inheritance."[9] Waymeyer summarizes how most amillennialists view Revelation 20:1–3:

> According to amillennialism, the binding of Satan in Revelation 20:1–3 took place at the first coming of Christ, and his imprisonment in the abyss extends throughout the present age, concurrent with the millennial reign of Jesus. Rather than describing a future event that will occur at the Second

---

[7] Ibid., 94-95. See R. Fowler White, "Reexamining the Evidence for Recapitulation in Rev. 20:1–10," *Westminster Theological Journal* 51 (Fall 1989): 319–44 for a more detailed argumentation for this view.

[8] Sam Storms, *Kingdom Come: The Amillennial Alternative* (Ross-shire, Scotland: Mentor Imprint, 2013), 431 (emphasis in the original).

[9] Ibid., 441. An argument against this view would be the massive conversion of the Gentiles of Nineveh during Jonah's ministry. A large number of Gentiles received the forgiveness of sins and a divine inheritance, and yet this was done before Satan is bound—according to Storms—occurring during the first coming of Jesus. No "binding of Satan" was necessary for God to do this great grace work among these Gentiles, nor was He hindered any by Satan not yet being bound in the abyss.

Coming, then, Satan's binding was accomplished by Christ when He conquered the devil through His death and resurrection during His earthly ministry. In this way, amillennialism asserts that the thousand-year binding of Satan extends from the time of the first coming of Christ to the time of His second coming and is therefore a present reality.[10]

The alternate position to the preconsummationist view Powell calls postconsummationism:

In this view the events in verses [Rev. 20:] 1–6 *follow* the second coming of Christ depicted in 19:11–21. Thus it involves chronological progression between the two passages. This view is essentially premillennial. The post-consummationist-progressive-premillennial viewpoint holds these four tenets. (1) The binding of Satan is yet future; it will take place when Christ returns. (2) The one thousand years are a literal period in which Christ will reign on earth from Jerusalem and with His people. (3) Satan will be loosed for a brief period at the end of the millennium, and this will be followed by the resurrection and judgment of the wicked at the Great White Throne judgment. (4) The new heavens and the new earth will be created after the millennium, that is a thousand years after Christ's second coming.[11]

---

[10] Matt Waymeyer, *Amillennialism and the Age to Come: A Premillennial Critique of the Two Age Model* (Kress Biblical Resources: 2016), 179. See also Samuel E. Waldron, *The End Times Made Simple: How Could Everyone Be So Wrong about Biblical Prophecy?* (Amityville, NY: Calvary Press, 2003), 94– 95; William Hendriksen, *More Than Conquerors: An Interpretation of the Book of Revelation* (Grand Rapids: Baker Books, 1967), 187–88. Waymeyer, *Amillennialism and the Age to Come,* 179, footnote #10 adds: "Although most amillennialists emphasize that the binding of Satan was accomplished specifically through the death and resurrection of Christ, others believe this binding began earlier when Jesus triumphed over Satan by resisting his temptations in the wilderness (Matt. 4:1–11; Luke 4:1–13) (Donald Garlington, "Reigning with Christ: Revelation 20:1–6 and the Question of the Millennium," *R&R* 6, no. 2 [Spring 1997]: 91; Anthony Hoekema, *The Bible and the Future* [Grand Rapids: Eerdmans Publishing, 1979], 229; Floyd E. Hamilton, *The Basis of Millennial Faith* [Grand Rapids: Eerdmans Publishing, 1955], 130–31; Hendriksen, *More Than Conquerors,* 187)."

[11] Powell, "Progression versus Recapitulation in Revelation 20:1–6," 95 (emphasis in the original). Powell adds in support of this position, "The current article presents three arguments in defense of premillennialism that have often been overlooked. These concern (a) the imprisonment of Satan compared with imprisonment and binding imagery mentioned elsewhere in Revelation and the New Testament, (b) the reign of the saints in 20:4–6 compared with the saints' reign mentioned elsewhere in Revelation, and (c) the significance of the accusative case for the extent of time in

The Lie

Whether or not Satan is already imprisoned in the abyss or that this awaits Jesus' return to earth is not a minor theological issue or just a hotly debated topic among debaters. So much importance is attached to these promises from God, which leads to our next biblical truth:

<u>New Testament Premillennial Doctrinal Truth #4</u>: *Scripture repeatedly shows that Satan is not currently bound in the abyss but will be when Jesus Christ returns to earth to reign in the thousand-year Millennial Kingdom (Rev. 20:1–3), at which conclusion Satan "must be released from the abyss for a short while."*

INITIAL CONSIDERATIONS OF WHAT BEING IN THE ABYSS REQUIRES

Whether Satan currently resides in the abyss or not in Revelation 20:1–3 strongly factors into the argumentation from both the amillennial and premillennial side; there is simply no way to avoid this, other than to totally ignore it, as do Gentry and Wellum in *Kingdom Through Covenant*.[12] It is staggering that in an almost 850-page book the Scripture index (848) lists *not even one reference* from Revelation 19–20, the two chapters that reveal the most biblical truths about the return and reign of the Lord Jesus Christ. What makes this even more egregious is the subtitle of their book: *A Biblical-Theological Understanding of the Covenants*. This would be similar to writing an 850-page biblical theology on the Genesis flood account, and yet going to the Scripture index and finding *not even one* reference cited from Genesis 6–9. Obviously, whether or not Satan is currently bound plays no more importance in Gentry and Wellum's eschatology than does anything else in these chapters; or to word this differently, it is evident that Revelation 19–20 plays no role whatsoever in the supposed biblical theology presented in *Kingdom Through Covenant*. For those who

---

reference to the thousand years" (ibid., 97– 98). Michael J. Vlach, "The Kingdom of God and the Millennium," *The Master's Seminary Journal* 23/2 (Fall 2012): 244, is a representative of such a position: "The events of Rev. 20:1–10 follow the second coming of Jesus described in Rev. 19:11. There is sequential progression, not recapitulation in this section."

[12] See Peter J. Gentry and Stephen J. Wellum, *Kingdom Through Covenant: A Biblical-Theological Understanding of the Covenants* (Wheaton, IL: Crossway, 2012).

actually deal with whether or not Satan is presently bound, what often is omitted—sometimes by both sides—but that should be a key beginning point of such a study is this: What does the Bible reveal that are the requirements for being in the abyss?

One of Storms'—and other amillennialists'—main attacks against the premillennial position is what folly they consider it to be for the abyss to be a real, actual, spatial place, and defining it thusly imposes "a rigidly wooden and artificial structure on symbolism that it simply isn't designed to sustain,"[13] and in viewing the abyss as actually a place one must interpret it "in an overly literalistic manner."[14] Storms asserts that "if the premillennialist insists on saying that Satan's being cast into the abyss in Revelation 20 must be interpreted in a literal, spatial way," he must also believe, among other such items listed, the following in order to be consistent in their woefully mistaken theology: (1) the angel was physically holding a literal key that could literally lock and unlock the pit; (2) the angel was holding a literal chain with material links that could be measured; (3) the angel literally grabbed the devil and wrestled him into submission and threw him into this pit; and (4) then questions as to whether Satan was a literal, physical serpent as he is called in verse 2.[15] In a similar way, amillennialist Jonathan Menn thinks he has the premillenialist also boxed in as one who must interpret the abyss in Revelation 20:1–3 as "an actual pit in the earth which has a physical lock and physical 'seal.'"[16]

Waymeyer shows the clear distinction in the two interpretive positions:

---

[13] Storms, *Kingdom Come*, 445.

[14] G. K. Beale, *The Book of Revelation*, NIGTC (Grand Rapids: Eerdmans Publishing, 1999), 987. Cited from Matt Waymeyer, "The Binding of Satan in Revelation 20," *MSJ* 26/1 (Spring 2015): 24, in the section entitled "The Significance of the Abyss" (24–30), who further writes: "Storms also rejects the idea of 'a localized geo-spatial place called the abyss' (*Kingdom Come*, 442), and according to Menn, the abyss in Rev. 20 is 'not spatial' but rather functions as a metaphor (*Biblical Eschatology*, 18)."

[15] Storms, *Kingdom Come*, 442–43.

[16] Menn, *Biblical Eschatology*, 18, 357.

The Lie

In contrast to the literal interpretation of premillennialism, Beale says the abyss should be understood as representing a spiritual dimension which exists alongside—and in the midst of—the earthly dimension. In this way, Beale sees the abyss in Rev. 20:1–3 as "one of the various metaphors representing the spiritual sphere in which the devil and his accomplices operate." For this reason, he rejects the idea that the abyss is spatially removed from the earth and that Satan's confinement in the abyss requires a complete abolition of his activity on earth. This view of the abyss enables the amillennialist to affirm that Satan prowls about like a roaring lion, engaged in the various activities ascribed to him in the New Testament, while simultaneously being confined to the abyss as described in Revelation 20.[17]

However, Waymeyer counters with this response to the amillennial attack against the way premillenialists understand the abyss:

The immediate problem with this argument concerns the false alternative it establishes between a literal and figurative interpretation of the abyss. According to the amillennialist, the abyss must be understood as either (a) a literal reference to a physical, bottomless pit which extends endlessly into the depths of the earth, or (b) a symbolic metaphor signifying "the spiritual sphere in which the devil and his accomplices operate." But this ignores the possibility that the abyss in Revelation 20 is a spirit prison for demonic beings, an actual location which imprisons them and prevents them from functioning outside of its confines. According to this third view, the abyss is neither a physical hole in the ground (the woodenly literal view) nor the spiritual sphere of demonic activity in general (the amillennial view), but

---

[17] Matt Waymeyer, "The Binding of Satan in Revelation 20," 24–25, footnote #28, cites Beale, *The Book of Revelation*, 987: "According to Beale, 'the abyss and the physical world are two different dimensions interpenetrating each other or existing alongside one another' (990), and elsewhere he refers to the abyss as 'the realm of demons over which Satan rules' (493). In a similar way, Venema refers to the abyss as 'the dwelling place of the demons' (Cornelis P. Venema, *The Promise of the Future* [Carlisle, PA: Banner of Truth, 2000], 316), and Storms refers to it as 'the abode of demons' (*Kingdom Come*, 429) and 'the source or abode of those demonic powers that are opposed to God' (478). But none of them emphasize the fact that the abyss is a 'prison' (Rev. 20:7). Other amillennialists are even less precise in their explanation of the abyss. For example, Hoekema says the abyss should "be thought of as a figurative description of the way in which Satan's activities will be curbed during the thousand-year period" (*The Bible and the Future*, 228), but this explanation communicates the effect of confinement in the abyss without defining what the abyss actually is."

rather *an actual location in the spiritual realm where evil spirits are confined and prevented from roaming free on earth.* A careful examination of ἄβυσσον indicates that this is indeed the meaning of this word in Revelation 20.[18]

As we will repeatedly see, the Bible offers many ways to prove that the above *italicized* conclusion is the proper way to understand the abyss. Also, it must be emphasized: Revelation 20:1–3 is part of *the overall visions* that God gave specifically to show and explain certain events (e.g., Rev. 1:1–2; 4:1). Such a vision that *God* used to communicate the imprisonment of Satan (Rev. 20:1–3) does not require that earthly, physical material be used to accomplish such a task, something Storms wrongly asserts must be present and the only means by which such a binding of Satan could occur, in his erroneous depiction of what the premillennialists' interpretation must entail.

Using Scripture is often presumed or sometimes stated by various authors as the basis of their theology, yet, upon closer examination, often this biblical requirement is not always the case. For instance, Sam Storms, in *Kingdom Come: The Amillennial Alternative*, in the subject index for "the meaning of the abyss," lists three page numbers (429, 478, 495).[19] For the first reference (429), Storms writes "The first interpretative task before us is the account of [Rev. 20:] 1–3 of Satan's imprisonment in the abyss. . ." He then uses footnote #7 to offer part of his understanding of what Satan's being currently bound in the abyss consists of:

> The word translated "abyss" occurs nine times in the New Testament, eight of which refer to the abode of demons. . . According to Robert Mounce, the abyss was thought of as "a vast subterranean cavern which served as a place of confinement for disobedient spirits awaiting judgment" (*The Book of Revelation* [Grand Rapids: Eerdmans,1977], 352). In Revelation 9:11 Satan is referred to as "the angel of the bottomless pit (or abyss), most likely because he is *in* the abyss, the place from which he dispatches his demonic hordes (9:1–3) and commissions the beast (11:7; 17:8). Although

---

[18] Ibid., 25 (emphasis in the original).

[19] Storms, *Kingdom Come*, 573.

this point should not be pressed, it may be that Satan is "in" the abyss precisely because he was consigned there and sealed therein at the inception of the present age, only to be released at its close. In other words, it may be that Satan is described as being "of the abyss" in 9:11 because that is the place of his current incarceration.[20]

In using biblical references in rebuttal to Storms' interpretation: First, Storms brings an interpretational judgment to Revelation 9:11 because Scripture does not require this to refer to Satan because the text does not designate him by name, and strong arguments exist that "Abaddon/Apollyon" most likely is a strong demon already imprisoned there by God—but not Satan himself.[21] Second, Storms holds that Satan and his angels are using the abyss as their functional home base to go and come as they please, because the abyss is "the place from which he [Satan] dispatches his demonic hordes (9:1–3) . . . ." Also, it would be difficult to explain that the abyss is "the place from which he dispatches his demonic hordes (9:1–3)," but yet deem it that Satan himself "is 'in' the abyss precisely because he was consigned there and sealed therein at the inception of the present age, only to be released at its close." Storms further concludes that Satan is described as being "'of the abyss' in 9:11 because that is the place of his current incarceration." From Storms' description arises substantial questions: If the abyss is a place from which Satan currently sends out his demonic hordes, and if so, why would Satan not go out from there himself (since he is sending others), since the abyss is also currently the place of Satan's incarceration? And we must ask—and will address this soon in this article—What then are the *biblical* requirements for such an incarceration?

For the second page under the subject index for "the meaning of the abyss" (478), Storms writes, "It may be that John's reference to the 'sea'

---

[20] Ibid., 429, fn. 7 (emphasis in the original).

[21] See Robert L. Thomas, *Revelation 8–22: An Exegetical Commentary* (Chicago: Moody Press, 1995), 37–39, for argumentation against Satan being the king over all the abyss, since nowhere in Scripture does Satan have any connection with the abyss until he is cast into it later. Thomas makes a significant case for identifying the leader of the abyss as some previously unnamed strong-ranking demon who is imprisoned by God and is unable to release himself from the abyss, until Jesus summons him and the other demons already in the abyss for their temporary release (Rev. 9:1–11).

is synonymous with 'the abyss,' the source and abode of those demonic powers that are opposed to God." That Storms considers the abyss to be "the *source* and *abode* of those demonic powers that are opposed to God" (emphasis added), is in keeping with his previous points, the abyss here consists of the home base of abiding and deploying of demonic powers by Satan. It should be regarded that nothing was noted about whether "the source and abode of those demonic powers that are opposed to God" refer to all of the demons or to only a subset of them. In the final page number for "the meaning of the abyss" (495), Storms writes, "This beast is later called 'the false prophet'" (16:13; 19:20; 20:10) and together with the dragon and the sea-beast forms the unholy trinity of the abyss."

The summary of Storms' references explaining the meaning of the abyss include: (1) Satan is the angel of the abyss, and presently is consigned and sealed there; (2) yet it is from the abyss that Satan sends out his demonic hordes; (3) the abyss is also the source and abode of the demonic powers who are opposed to God, but not necessarily their confinement there; and (4) finally, there will eventually be some form of the unholy trinity of the abyss that will play some role in some of the final eschatological events.

To show the vast difference between the approach espoused by Storms in *Kingdom Come* versus searching for and accepting the Bible definitions will be strikingly obvious, because in the Scripture index in *Kingdom Come*, not one of the necessary, pertinent Bible verses appear about the abyss—and remember, his subject index for his book already contains a subject called "the meaning of the abyss"—and yet his definition does not include *any* of the information from the Scriptural accounts that follow below.

To begin with, two other important matters must be considered: first, the only way we would know that hell, Hades or the abyss—or heaven—exist is because God chooses to reveal them and some of their descriptions, and if these Scriptural descriptions are not used and accepted, then it is *not God's definitions* being used. Second, as will be repeatedly shown scripturally, the Godhead alone has the authority over both Hades and the abyss—with Satan having absolutely no authority over it in even the slightest way.

Initially, the Bible reveals much about the eventual and ultimate punishment of evil spiritual beings, including in Matthew 25:41, when Jesus will tell the lost humans who are alive at His return to earth, "Then He will also say to those on His left, 'Depart from Me, accursed ones, *into the eternal fire which has been prepared for the devil and his angels*'" (emphasis added). Many humans will certainly spend eternity in hell, but God's original design for hell was for "the devil and his angels," usually referred to by their more common designation as "demons," and, as will be shown later in this article, *all* demons will eventually be confined in the abyss first, and then all of the demons will ultimately be cast into hell. We should also note that the Bible clearly depicts hell to be an actual place with spatial boundaries—not a spiritual condition. Although through the centuries there has been the erroneous belief in many people's understanding of what hell is, it should be emphasized that the Bible never presents Satan as reigning over hell as his abode. Once Jesus casts Satan into hell, the devil will be excruciatingly tormented there "forever and ever" (Rev. 20:10).

Concerning the abyss, we will begin with an important doctrine of what the abyss is not: the abyss is not the same as Hades, and this truth will connect with a future item in this article.[22] Hades is the place where the souls of the dead, unsaved humans reside at the present time, as Jesus revealed in Luke 16:19–29:

> "Now there was a certain rich man, and he habitually dressed in purple and fine linen, gaily living in splendor every day. And a certain poor man named Lazarus was laid at his gate, covered with sores, and longing to be

---

[22] Powell writes: "In Revelation only the demonic are related to the abyss; death and Hades are usually related to humanity. In 6:8 death and Hades are personalized and represent the judgment of death on [unsaved] humanity; death is the experience and hades is the destination. Death and hades are again used figuratively in 20:13–14 of those who dwell in hades and have experienced death as judgment. In the New Testament, hades is always the place of the unbelieving dead (Matt. 11:23; 16:18; 10:15; Luke 16:23; 2:27; Acts 2:31; Rev. 1:18; Rev. 6:8; 20:13–14), and is a realm from which they cannot escape" (Powell, "Progression versus Recapitulation in Revelation 20:1–6," 98–99).

fed with the crumbs which were falling from the rich man's table; besides, even the dogs were coming and licking his sores.

"Now it came about that the poor man died and he was carried away by the angels to Abraham's bosom; and the rich man also died and was buried.

"And in Hades he lifted up his eyes, being in torment, and saw Abraham far away, and Lazarus in his bosom. "And he cried out and said, 'Father Abraham, have mercy on me, and send Lazarus, that he may dip the tip of his finger in water and cool off my tongue; for I am in agony in this flame.'

"But Abraham said, 'Child, remember that during your life you received your good things, and likewise Lazarus bad things; but now he is being comforted here, and you are in agony. And besides all this, between us and you there is a great chasm fixed, in order that those who wish to come over from here to you may not be able, and that none may cross over from there to us.'

"And he said, 'Then I beg you, Father, that you send him to my father's house —for I have five brothers—that he may warn them, lest they also come to this place of torment.' "But Abraham said, 'They have Moses and the Prophets; let them hear them.'"

Among other things, we learn from the previous and following passages: (1) Hades is not the abyss; nothing about the abyss is mentioned here; (2) Hades is a real place ("this place of torment"), and not some sort of spiritual condition of anguish during one's life on earth that no longer existed at that time ("that during your life"), (Lk. 16:25, 29); (3) Hades is not hell; rather Hades is the temporary holding place of fallen human souls awaiting the Great White Throne Judgment, as seen in Revelation 20:13: "And the sea gave up the dead which were in it, and death and Hades gave up the dead which were in them; and they were judged, every one of them according to their deeds." (4) While Hades is not hell, it is nonetheless a place of torment ("being in torment"/ "for I am in agony in this flame"/ "lest they [the rich man's five brothers] come to this place of torment"). (5) Luke 16:26 reveals that those in Hades are separated and far removed from the wonderful abode of the redeemed: "And besides all this, between us and you there is a great chasm fixed, in order that those who wish to come over from here to you may not be able, and that none may cross over from there to us." Finally, (6) those in Hades are either 100% in Hades or they are not there at all; there is no middle ground of "sort of being" in Hades or sort of being on earth, such as being 50% in Hades 50% on earth. If one is in Hades, one is no longer on the earth; if one is still on the earth—no matter how horrific whatever pains befall them—that person is not in Hades. Those who believe the Bible as God's Word and their source of truth would receive these teachings from Jesus because no living human being has seen Hades or would even know from only a human perspective that it exists, nor know any of its characteristics. For the most part, Hades is not a point of contention between the amillennialists and premillennialists.

THE BIBLICAL DEFINITION AND REQUIREMENTS FOR BEING IN THE ABYSS

Just as with seeking the God-given definition of Hades and of hell, seeking to find the God-given definition and requirements should be done also for the abyss, and God's Word has much to say about the abyss. One's correct biblical definition of the abyss *must* include the following verses, or it will not match the revelation given by God. For instance, Luke 8:26–31 reveals several truths about the abyss, as seen by the resulting terror, questions, and pleas that one particular subset of demons had when they encountered the incarnate Jesus:

> And they sailed to the country of the Gerasenes, which is opposite Galilee. And when He had come out onto the land, He was met by a certain man from the city who was possessed with demons; and who had not put on any clothing for a long time, and was not living in a house, but in the tombs. And seeing Jesus, he cried out and fell before Him, and said in a loud voice, "What do I have to do with You, Jesus, Son of the Most High God? I beg You, do not torment me." For He had been commanding the unclean spirit to come out of the man. For it had seized him many times; and he was bound with chains and shackles and kept under guard; and yet he would burst his fetters and be driven by the demon into the desert.
> And Jesus asked him, "What is your name?"
> And he said, "Legion"; for many demons had entered him. And they were entreating Him not to command them to depart into the abyss.

Premillennialism In The New Testament: Five Biblically Doctrinal Truths

Waymeyer also states this quite striking result of his studies an essential core truth: "In discussing the incarceration of Satan in Revelation 20, most amillennialists do not even mention—much less comment on—the implications of Luke 8:31 for an accurate understanding of the abyss,"[23] yet they most certainly should examine any pertinent passages on the abyss—as is required for any other biblical doctrine, because to omit any of the characteristics about the abyss as revealed by God in Scripture certainly weakens their interpretation elsewhere of what the abyss consists of as well as its purpose. And this is important and noteworthy: *not even one* of the following Bible verses describing the abyss made it into Storms' *Kingdom Come* Scripture index—nor do any of the truths revealed there. As we will see, it is not only Luke 8 verses that amillennialists such as Storms omits; there are more Scripture verses that God gave to describe the abyss that are not included in the Scripture index of *Kingdom Come*, nor that he used to define the abyss.

From the Luke 8:26–31 passage we learn, among other things, about the abyss: (1) Demons are fully cognizant that the abyss exists, and that it is an actual place, and that if they departed into the abyss, it would be a place of horrible torment for them (Luke 8:28); (2) The demons knew that Jesus–even in His incarnation–possessed the authority to "command them to depart into the abyss" (Luke 8:31); (3) It is evident that the demons knew that as long as they were on earth, they had not yet "depart[ed] into the abyss." (4) As with hell and Hades, the abyss belongs to God alone—not to Satan—and the only way into either Hades or the abyss is if the Godhead or one of its members puts them there, and the only way out of Hades or the abyss is if God Himself, or one of God's holy angels commanded to do so, such as is seen in the opening verses of Revelation 9. (5) Demons cannot be in two places at the same time; as with human and Hades, this is also an "either/or" category: demons are either 100% operative with access to earth in the demonic realm, or they are 100% imprisoned in the abyss, completely removed

---

[23] Waymeyer, *Amillennialism and the Age to Come*, 185, footnote #39, lists four popular amillennial works (Riddlebarger, *A Case for Amillennialism*; Venema, *The Promise of the Future*; Hoekema, *The Bible and the Future*; Storms, *Kingdom Come*).

from earth. (6) The parallel account in Matthew 8:29 explains the demons rightful fear that they have: "And behold, they cried out, saying, 'What do we have to do with You, Son of God? Have You come here to torment us before *the time*?'" (emphasis added). Although the particulars are not explained at this point of what or when "the time" will be, demons know that they all await a judgment from Jesus, which helps explain James 2:19: "Demons believe and shudder/tremble" (present tense)—and they have good reason to shudder/tremble on an on-going basis. Waymeyer summarizes the importance of Luke 8 thusly:

> [T]he narrative in Luke 8 indicates that confinement in the abyss involves the complete removal of demonic activity and influence upon the earth. This can be seen in the request of the demons in verse 31. The reason for the demons' request was not because they were so determined to kill the swine. The reason for their request was because imprisonment in the abyss would have cut them off from having any influence in this world—at least as long as they were *in* the abyss—whereas a departure into the swine would allow them to continue to roam free and wreak havoc on the earth. This indicates that these evil spirits could either be imprisoned in the abyss or they could be prowling about the earth—engaged in demonic activities—but they could not be both.[24]

In order to find out other characteristics about the abyss, we must look to other verses that describe the abyss without actually using the word "abyss," and remembering that, along with the Luke 8 and Matthew 8 passages, none of the following verses factor into Storms' definition of what the abyss entails, because none of the following verses are in the Scripture Index in *Kingdom Come*. Initially, Scripture reveals that some subset(s) of demons are currently in the abyss, while others are free (presently) to do their evil activity, as seen in 1 Peter 3:18–20:

> For Christ also died for sins once for all, the just for the unjust, in order that He might bring us to God, having been put to death in the flesh, but made alive in the spirit; in which also He went and made proclamation to the spirits now in prison, who once were disobedient, when the patience of

---

[24] Ibid., 185 (emphasis his).

God kept waiting in the days of Noah, during the construction of the ark, in which a few, that is, eight persons, were brought safely through the water.

We see from this passage (1) First Peter 3:19–20 reveals that there are some demonic spirits "now in prison;" (2) this particular subset of demons are already "now in prison" because their particular acts of disobedience occurred during the days of Noah, but before the Flood; (3) the Godhead may have other demons already imprisoned in the abyss for other heinous sins that they committed, but the Bible is silent as to whether other demons likewise are currently in the abyss; (4) obviously, not every demon is in the abyss yet. Other demons, besides the ones as the (Legion) in Luke 8, are not in the abyss but are currently actively sinning on earth, helping to achieve some of "the schemes of the devil," as Paul warned and exhorted in regard to spiritual warfare in Ephesians 6:10–12;

> Finally, be strong in the Lord, and in the strength of His might. Put on the full armor of God, that you may be able to stand firm against the schemes of the devil. For our struggle is not against flesh and blood, but against the rulers, against the powers, against the world forces of this darkness, against the spiritual forces of wickedness in the heavenly places.

(5) The demons described in Ephesians 6 are allowed—under God's sovereignty and authority—to currently carry out demonic activities that those demons already in the prison of the abyss are no longer permitted to do.

Next, Second Peter 2:4–5 describes the abyss thusly: "For if God did not spare angels when they sinned, but cast them into hell and committed them to pits of darkness, reserved for judgment; and did not spare the ancient world, but preserved Noah, a preacher of righteousness, with seven others, when He brought a flood upon the world of the ungodly . . ." From these verses, we see two vital truths: (1) All demons sin, but some demons have sinned to such a heinous degree that God has already removed them from the world, "cast them into hell [*tartarus*] and committed them to pits of darkness, reserved for judgment;"[25] (2)

---

[25] See John MacArthur and Richard Mayhue, *Biblical Doctrine: A Systematic Summary of*

"reserved for judgment" means that the demons who are already imprisoned and are tortured in the abyss have not yet received their ultimate judgment, which clearly indicates that a future and final judgment past this initial incarceration remains for them and ultimately the entire demonic world, at some undisclosed time in the future.

Jude 6 adds this in reference to the abyss: "And angels who did not keep their own domain, but abandoned their proper abode, He has kept in eternal bonds under darkness for the judgment of the great day." Jude 6 reveals that *God Himself*—not Satan— "has kept" [these demons in the abyss] "in eternal bonds under darkness," and thus refutes Storms' derisive and erroneous appraisal of what the premillennial understanding of what the binding of Satan in a chain must entail in Revelation 20:1–3, as well as what he considers the sheer folly of such a concept as a spiritual being—such as Satan—could possibly be bound in the abyss.[26] As we have seen before, the Godhead is in charge of the abyss—not Satan. The perfect tense used for "has kept" [τετήρηκεν] depicts this strong judgment of God done to this particular set of demons as having occurred in the past and is still continuing to the present day, without any interruption of their confinement in God's prison of the abyss.[27]

So, from the biblical record concerning demons and the abyss, God reveals and defines the abyss thusly: (1) some demons are already in prison in the abyss and are currently being tormented by God (1 Pet. 3:19); (2) other demons who are not presently in the abyss are organized into a hierarchy, strong, powerful, and active and are part of the present spiritual warfare against the redeemed (Eph. 6:10–12). The demons who are already imprisoned in the abyss play no part in any capacity against the redeemed; (3) demons currently in the abyss are "cast into [temporary] hell" [*tartarus*] and God Himself "committed them to pits of darkness," where they are reserved for judgment until their ultimate and

---

Bible Truth (Wheaton: Crossway, 2017), 845–46, who explain that *tartarus*, used only here in the NT, is not the lake of fire hell of Revelation 20, but rather became the terms the Jews used to explain where some of the fallen angels were sent to endure their preliminary torment, which, from its usage, thus equates it with the abyss.

[26] Contra Storms, *Kingdom Come*, 442–43.

[27] D. Edmund Hiebert, *Second Peter and Jude: An Expositional Commentary* (Greenville, SC: Unusual Publications, 1989), 234–35.

final judgment that is repeatedly promised in Scripture; (4) demons currently in the abyss, "He [God/the Godhead] has kept in eternal bonds under darkness for the judgment of the great day"—and they are removed from and no longer have access to or are operative on earth. (5) Storms cites no biblical references that indicate or depict that the demons, who if currently confined in the abyss, can exist or function in the world, or that they are now working in the world in some weakened form than what they were previously able to do, after the crucifixion of Jesus. (6) As with humans in Hades, so it is true with the demons and the abyss: demons are either 100% in the abyss, or they are not in the abyss at all; no other options are available to them. (7) Finally, all the verses used to describe the abyss have God alone as master and sovereign over all who enter into or ever depart from the abyss—which is important—because not one singular verse cited depicts Satan as master of the abyss, and "the place from which he dispatches his demonic hordes."[28]

One final thought on this section must be emphasized: it must be remembered that although God, through His sovereignty and allowance, has currently granted Satan enormous power (Jude 9), Satan, at his base essence is nonetheless still and only a demon, and is the leader of "his angels," the remaining demons (Matt. 25:41)—but that is the complete limits of his power. So whatever is true about demons being imprisoned in the abyss must be true for Satan when he is imprisoned in the abyss in Revelation 20:1–3, and when this is done, the same characteristics and horrors of the abyss will be true for him as well—with no exception.

So, succinctly summarized from the verses of Scripture, here are the necessary biblical requirements and characteristics for the demons to be in abyss:

(1) Removed by God from "the playing field" of earth and instead are confined in prison (1 Pet. 3:19)
(2) Currently under torment (Luke 8:28)
(3) In a temporary hell [*tartartus*] (2 Pet. 2:4)
(4) Committed to pits of darkness (2 Pet. 2:4)

---

[28] Contra Storms, *Kingdom Come*, 429, fn. 7.

(5) Kept by God in eternal bonds under darkness from which they cannot escape (Jude 6)
(6) God specifically keeping them in this abyss of torment for the judgment of the great day (Matt. 8:29; 2 Pet. 2:4; Jude 6)
(7) Also, nothing from these verses indicates anything about those demons who are cast into the abyss as merely having a reduction of their spiritual strength while still remaining on earth and committing the same sins that other demons do.

Storms' understanding of what the abyss is, in *Kingdom Come*: (1) has none of the following verses in his Scripture index; (2) consequently, he does not have a true biblical definition of what the abyss consists of; (3) nothing in Scripture gives any evidence that the abyss belongs to Satan, that he is there now, or that he uses the abyss to send out his demonic hordes; (4) and without a proper understanding of what the abyss is, one cannot hope to have a proper biblical understanding of what Satan's being bound in the abyss means (Rev. 20:1–3), or the correct interpretation of Satan's later release from the abyss 1,000 years later (Rev. 20:7). Simply stated, Storms' presentation of the meaning of what being imprisoned in the abyss entails absolutely does not align with the biblical definition and requirements as given by God in His Word.

WHEN DID OR WHEN WILL THE BINDING OF SATAN IN THE ABYSS OCCUR?

Multiple verses exist about the future judgment of Satan and his angels, and as we previously determined, we need to examine (1) whether the judgment occurred in the past at Jesus' crucifixion and death—the most popular amillennial view—and thus has already occurred historically, or (2) whether the judgment will happen at the Second Coming of Jesus, since this is the dividing line of interpretation for Bible-believing scholars, and/or Christians, as we saw earlier in this article. Sadly, here is a novel idea for some: we should begin with what *the Bible* indicates about whether or not this prophesied judgment has already occurred, such as at the death of Jesus, or if this judgment still awaits a future fulfillment. Also, it must be answered: if one believes what the Bible reveals as the characteristics of Hades—which is the only way we would know anything about Hades, then it *must* be explained why others would not receive/believe/accept what this same Bible teaches regarding the abyss—of which the existence and characteristics are also revealed. Therefore, it must be explained why if one accepts what the Bible teaches regarding Hades, one does not also accept what the same Bible teaches about the abyss, including as a very essential part of this, the time of the occurrence of the promised imprisonment in the abyss.

Other than having a predetermined conclusion and hermeneutic already and repeatedly forced upon the text, the Bible is explicit about when the final judgment will occur. Isaiah 24–27, the section often referred to as "The Apocalypse of Isaiah," with multiple references to the earth and its judgment and the Lord's return and reign, contains this biblical revelation from God by means of Isaiah 24:21–23:

> So it will happen in that day, that the LORD will punish the host of heaven, on high, and the kings of the earth, on earth. And they will be gathered together like prisoners in the dungeon [pit], and will be confined in prison; and after many days they will be punished.
> Then the moon will be abashed and the sun ashamed, for the LORD of hosts will reign on Mount Zion and in Jerusalem, and His glory will be before His elders.

As noted earlier, it must be remembered that Satan, although he is currently massively strong (Jude 9), is nonetheless in his base essence a fallen angel, and thus part of the "heavenly host" that is referred to four times in the Bible, with two times being referred to as the evil part of the heavenly host, namely Satan and his demons: In Deuteronomy 17:3, God rebuked the wilderness generation for their sins that they "have gone and served other gods and worshiped them, or the sun or the moon or *any of the heavenly host, which I have not commanded . . .*" Centuries later, Jeremiah 19:13 reveals, as the Babylonian exile was at hand, part of the sins of the kings and the people: "And the houses of Jerusalem and the houses of the kings of Judah will be defiled like the place Tophet, because of all the houses on whose rooftops *they burned sacrifices to all the heavenly host* and poured out libations to other gods."

The usage for the good heavenly host is seen in passages such as Nehemiah 9:6:

> "You alone are the LORD. You have made the heavens, the heaven of heavens with all their host, the earth and all that is on it, the seas and all that is in them. You do give life to all of them and the heavenly host bows down before You."

Luke 2:13 provides an incredibly worship-evoking and proper response to some of the shepherds of Bethlehem in announcing the birth of the Messiah: "And suddenly there appeared with the angel a multitude of the heavenly host praising God, and saying . . ."

So when God proclaims in Isaiah 24:21, "So it will happen in that day, that the LORD will punish the host of heaven, on high," this clearly refers to the evil part of the host on high or heavenly hosts, namely "the devil and his angels" (Matt. 25:41). There never is any need for God to judge the holy part of the hosts of heaven because they never sin, while the wicked part of the heavenly host—who can function only within whatever boundaries that God allows—never stop sinning. Isaiah 24:21–23 is one of the God-given descriptions from the Bible as to when the day of judgment that the demons of Matthew 8/Luke 8/James 2 fear, and it connects with and will occur at the Second Coming of Jesus Christ to earth—not as having occurred during His incarnation or after at His eternally important work accomplished by Jesus on the cross.[29]

In order for one's understanding of this future judgment to be biblically accurate, one's eschatology must include: (1) the initial defeat, imprisonment, and punishment of the wicked host of heaven on high and the kings of the earth on earth occurring at the same time; (2) these will be gathered together in a prison, (3) after many days they will be judged with a second, eternal judgment that begins with them being cast into hell, and (4) the Messiah must return in/with the glory of God. If your eschatological system does not contain these items, it does not match the biblical account:

---

[29] Contra Storms, *Kingdom Come*, 441.

An Old Testament backdrop for an intermediate kingdom is also found in Isaiah 24. The first twenty verses of Isaiah 24 describe global judgments on the earth for transgressing God's laws (Isa. 24:5). Then a two-stage judgment of God's enemies is mentioned in 24:21–23: "On that day the LORD will punish the host of heaven in heaven, and the kings of the earth, on the earth. They will be gathered together as prisoners in a pit; they will be shut up in prison, and after many days they will be punished. Then the moon will be confounded." Both evil spiritual forces ("the host of heaven") and evil human forces ("kings of the earth") will be judged. There will also be an incarceration. They will be "gathered together as prisoners in a pit," and "shut up in prison." But then we are told, "After many days they will be punished." The order of the events here is imprisonment for many days and the punishment. The "after many days" phrase coincides well with the concept of an intermediate kingdom of a thousand years in Revelation 20, which says that Satan will be bound in the Abyss for a thousand years, then released for a short time, and finally sentenced to the lake of fire (Rev. 20:1–3, 7).[30]

One other very important point is that Isaiah 24:21–22 reveals, "So it will happen in that day, that the LORD will punish the host of heaven, on high, and the kings of the earth, on earth. And they will be gathered together like prisoners in the dungeon [pit], and will be confined in prison; and after many days they will be punished." At this unique judgment of those aligned against Jesus at His return, Scripture verses given later reveal that the kings of the earth and those human beings with them by this time already (1) having worshiped Satan and the Antichrist (Rev. 13:4), (2) having received "the 666 mark of the beast" (Rev. 13:16–18; 14:9–11), (3) having thoroughly rejected the love of the truth offered to them that would have led to their salvation (2 Thess. 2:10), and (4) some having played various parts in the deaths of the martyrs of Revelation 6:9–11. It seems from the Isaiah 24 passage, instead of departing to the normal abode of the dead human spirits, namely Hades, the kings of the earth and their human followers will all be slain, and then they all will be gathered together with the entire fallen host of heaven for additional punishment in the abyss. If one argued that this is

---

[30] MacArthur and Mayhue, *Biblical Doctrine*, 890.

not the method that God uses in the Bible, God can do as He pleases; it should be remembered that God can put His defeated enemies wherever He wants them and whenever He wants to put them there. Also, to be considered are Jesus' statements of the uniqueness of the Tribulation, as seen in Matthew 24:21-22: "for then there will be a great tribulation, such as has not occurred since the beginning of the world until now, nor ever shall. And unless those days had been cut short, no life would have been saved; but for the sake of the elect those days shall be cut short." Further, in a section of Scripture where Jesus first tells of His death (Matt. 16:21), He concludes this same chapter with His promised return, in harmony with the glory of God from Isaiah 24:23, as revealed in Matthew 16:27: "For the Son of Man is going to come in the glory of His Father with His angels; and WILL THEN RECOMPENSE EVERY MAN ACCORDING TO HIS DEEDS."

None of these doctrinal truths taken from Scripture about what the abyss entails apply to Satan at the present time, nor were they received—nor prophesied to occur—at the death of Jesus, because not even one of these events occurred at that time, as revealed in Isaiah 24:21–23:

(1) In that day, that the LORD will punish the host of heaven, on high, and the kings of the earth, on earth, imprisoning them in great torment
(2) They will be gathered together like prisoners in the dungeon [pit]
(3) They will be confined in prison
(4) After many days they will be punished
(5) Then the moon will be abashed and the sun ashamed, for the LORD of hosts will reign on Mount Zion and in Jerusalem, and His glory will be before His elders.

Further, in harmony with previous references, all of the following items will apply specifically to Jesus at His Second Coming to earth, as disclosed in Matthew 24:29– 31:

But immediately after the tribulation of those days THE SUN WILL BE DARKENED, AND THE MOON WILL NOT GIVE ITS LIGHT, AND THE STARS WILL FALL from the sky, and the powers of the heavens will be shaken, and then the sign of the Son of Man will appear in the sky, and then all the tribes of the earth will mourn, and they will see the SON OF MAN COMING ON THE CLOUDS OF THE SKY with power and great glory. And He will send forth His angels with A GREAT TRUMPET and THEY WILL GATHER TOGETHER His elect from the four winds, from one end of the sky to the other.

In Matthew 24:29 "and the powers of the heavens will be shaken" cannot be referring to the sun, moon, or stars, because they are already mentioned in this text; rather these powers of the heavens are those designated in Isaiah 24:21, which is another reference to the evil part of the heavenly host who will receive their temporary confinement at the return of Jesus—per Isaiah 24:21–22: "So it will happen in that day, that the LORD will punish the host of heaven, on high, and the kings of the earth, on earth. And they will be gathered together like prisoners in the dungeon [pit], and will be confined in prison; and after many days they will be punished." The "many days" of Isaiah 24:22 is not found in the Matthew 24:29–31 passage, but Scripture does not need to be repeated each time to make it true; God's declaration in Isaiah 24:22 is totally sufficient. But we must remember also, God's revelatory eschatology has an initial time of imprisonment of the kings of the earth and their followers on earth imprisoned together with the fallen and now conquered heavenly host—which will include Satan as one of the detainees, before their final and ultimate judgment before Jesus, "after many days."

TWO OF THE DIFFERENT ACCOUNTS OF THE ACTUAL TRIUMPHAL ENTRY AND THEIR SIGNIFICANCE

Zechariah 14:1–9 and Revelation 19:11–20:3 are two of other Scripture accounts that describe the true Triumphal Entry of Jesus. Zechariah 14:1–8 prophesies and reveals:

> Behold, a day is coming for the LORD when the spoil taken from you will be divided among you. For I will gather all the nations against Jerusalem to battle, and the city will be captured, the houses plundered, the women ravished, and half of the city exiled, but the rest of the people will not be

cut off from the city. Then the LORD will go forth and fight against those nations, as when He fights on a day of battle. And in that day His feet will stand on the Mount of Olives, which is in front of Jerusalem on the east; and the Mount of Olives will be split in its middle from east to west by a very large valley, so that half of the mountain will move toward the north and the other half toward the south. And you will flee by the valley of My mountains, for the valley of the mountains will reach to Azel; yes, you will flee just as you fled before the earthquake in the days of Uzziah king of Judah.

Then the LORD, my God, will come, and all the holy ones with Him! And it will come about in that day that there will be no light; the luminaries will dwindle. For it will be a unique day which is known to the LORD, neither day nor night, but it will come about that at evening time there will be light. [Harmonizes with Isa. 24:23; Matt. 25:29] And it will come about in that day that living waters will flow out of Jerusalem, half of them toward the eastern sea and the other half toward the western sea; it will be in summer as well as in winter.

When the Lord Messiah Jesus returns to earth with the glory of God, Zechariah 14:9 contains this very crucial explanatory doctrine: "And the LORD will be king over all the earth; in that day the LORD will be the only one, and His name the only one." Not one of the enemies of God—neither human nor demonic—will ever be ruling at that time because Jesus Himself, at the time of His promised return, will have defeated and imprisoned all His enemies, as we have seen already in Isaiah 24:21–23 and shall see in other accounts. Thus, any of the titles that Satan currently has will be eternally removed from him as "in that day" begins with his initial judgment and confinement in the torment of the abyss for many days, and then, eventually, with his being thrown into hell forever. So "in that day" will eventually/ultimately continue into eternity. Yet the Bible repeatedly indicates that Satan *currently* holds titles and capacities that were attributed to him *after* the death of Jesus but *before* His Second Coming to earth, because once Jesus returns to earth to reign, Satan's titles and capabilities will be permanently removed, and *never* can Satan retrieve even one of them, and this is one of the strongest biblical supports for Satan currently *not* being imprisoned in the abyss.

The disclosure of the real Triumphal Entry in Revelation 19:11–20:3 can be rightly connected with what God reveals in this passage, with first the unveiling of Christ Jesus with the attributes of God, beginning in Revelation 19:11–16:

> And I saw heaven opened; and behold, a white horse, and He who sat upon it is called Faithful and True; and in righteousness He judges and wages war. And His eyes are a flame of fire, and upon His head are many diadems; and He has a name written upon Him which no one knows except Himself. And He is clothed with a robe dipped in blood; and His name is called The Word of God. And the armies which are in heaven, clothed in fine linen, white and clean, were following Him on white horses. And from His mouth comes a sharp sword, so that with it He may smite the nations; and He will rule them with a rod of iron; and He treads the wine press of the fierce wrath of God, the Almighty.
> And on His robe and on His thigh He has a name written, "KING OF KINGS AND LORD OF LORDS."

Revelation 19:17–21 continues the account:

> And I saw an angel standing in the sun; and he cried out with a loud voice, saying to all the birds which fly in midheaven, "Come, assemble for the great supper of God; in order that you may eat the flesh of kings and the flesh of commanders and the flesh of mighty men and the flesh of horses and of those who sit on them and the flesh of all men, both free men and slaves, and small and great."
> And I saw the beast and the kings of the earth and their armies, assembled to make war against Him who sat upon the horse, and against His army. And the beast was seized, and with him the false prophet who performed the signs in his presence, by which he deceived those who had received the mark of the beast and those who worshiped his image; these two were thrown alive into the lake of fire which burns with brimstone. And the rest were killed with the sword which came from the mouth of Him who sat upon the horse, and all the birds were filled with their flesh.

Although God purposely chose not to include every event, we know from Isaiah 24:21–22 that when kings of the earth are being defeated by Jesus, so too occurs the defeat of the totality of the evil part of the host of heaven that will transpire at Jesus' return in Isaiah 24:21–22:

So it will happen in that day, that the LORD will punish the host of heaven, on high, and the kings of the earth, on earth. And they will be gathered together like prisoners in the dungeon [pit], and will be confined in prison; and after many days they will be punished.

Then, in keeping with Satan being head of the evil part of the host of heaven, he too is included in this prophesied judgment of Isaiah 24:22; Satan also "will be gathered together like prisoners in the dungeon [pit] and will be confined in prison"—including Satan—as Revelation 20:1–3 reveals *and* requires:

And I saw an angel coming down from heaven, having the key of the abyss and a great chain in his hand. And he laid hold of the dragon, the serpent of old, who is the devil and Satan, and bound him for a thousand years, and threw him into the abyss, and shut it and sealed it over him, so that he should not deceive the nations any longer, until the thousand years were completed; after these things he must be released for a short time.

The biblical story is far from over at this point, but in keeping with all the other verses we have seen regarding the return of the Lord, when Jesus reigns, as seen earlier in Zechariah 14:9, He will be the only One and His name the only one. Consequently, this would mean that, among other things: (1) Satan will no longer ever again hold the title "the god of this age" (2 Cor. 4:4); that age will have ended, when Jesus begins His reign on earth during the Millennial Kingdom. (2) First John 5:19 clearly sets forth this for the present time, under the authoritative sovereignty of God: "We know that we are of God, and the whole world lies in the power of the evil one"—but never again will even the tiniest part of the world be under the power of the evil once Jesus reigns. (3) Add to this 1 John 4:4: "You are from God, little children, and have overcome them; because greater is He who is in you than he who is in the world"—not greater than he who is already in the abyss. As was true for the demons of Luke 8, so it is true for Satan, as a member of the evil part of the heavenly host, that Satan cannot be in two places at once: if Satan is in the world, he is not in the abyss; if Satan is in the abyss, he is not in the world. (4) When Jesus returns, Satan will no longer be considered "your adversary, the devil," who "prowls about like a roaring lion seeking someone to devour" (Job 1-2)—which the Godhead presently permits him to do—again under God's protective sovereignty (see Job 1-2). First Peter 5:9 denotes the playing field of such a spiritual battle for believers: "But resist him, firm in your faith, knowing that the same experiences of suffering are being accomplished by your brethren who are in the world"—but never again will resisting him be necessary once Satan is imprisoned in the abyss. (5) Remembering the summary promise of Zechariah 14:9, at the true Triumphal Entry: "And the LORD will be king over all the earth; in that day the LORD will be the only one, and His name the only one," yet before this, for the present time, Ephesians 2:2 describes Satan as "the prince of the power of the air," a depiction true of Satan now, but one that cannot be true when Jesus reigns, because if this verse still were to be true for Satan *after* Jesus returns to earth, Jesus would not be truly the only king over all the earth, and His name the only one. One should not confuse that Jesus' reigning alone means that He will not fulfill the promises to the redeemed by apportioning the rewards to reign with Him (e.g., Rev. 2:26–27; 3:21), which He will fulfill into eternity. So if even *only one evil prince* were allowed to do his demonic work after Jesus' return to earth, contrary to the commands of Jesus, then the doctrine of Zechariah 14:9 would be nullified. Satan's hierarchy of the demonic assemblage whereby he presently operates some of his "schemes of the devil," as we saw earlier in Ephesians 6:10–12, *cannot* function as they did before/do now because "in that day the LORD will be the only one, and His name the only one." Currently there exists another prince with his demonic hoards that he uses, but he will never again be "the prince of the power of the air" (Eph. 2:2), once he is imprisoned in the abyss.

One final connective truth with this, from what Jesus revealed in Mark 4:13–15:

> And He said to them, "Do you not understand this parable? And how will you understand all the parables? The sower sows the word. And these are the ones who are beside the road where the word is sown; and when they hear, immediately Satan comes and takes away the word which has been sown in them.

This parable reveals that whenever the Word of God is sown, Satan—at the present time—immediately comes and attempts to take away the Word which has been sown—but this will not be true for him once he will be imprisoned in the abyss. In fact, one of the main reasons that Satan will be in the abyss—as it relates to earth— is that he will no longer deceive the nations as long as he is in the abyss, nor will he have the capacity to take away the word which has been sown in them (Rev. 20:3, 7–8). Neither will Satan—when imprisoned in the abyss—be allowed to "blind the minds of the unbelieving" (2 Cor. 4:3–4). Clearly these present truths about Satan and the titles attributed to him are applicable only under God's sovereignty, and as the Bible reveals, these titles and capabilities certainly occur even *after* the death and ascension of Jesus, but *before* His return in the glory of the Father (Matt. 16:27), after which God renders Satan's power inactive. At the return of the Lord Jesus, for truly at that time and into eternity: "And the LORD will be king over all the earth; in that day the LORD will be the only one, and His name the only one (Zech. 14:9).

Further emphasis should be placed on exactly where Satan will be when the Lord Jesus Christ returns and what that means as far as restricting him:

> The location of the devil's imprisonment makes it especially clear that the confinement of Revelation 20:1–3 will prevent any satanic activity and influence on earth during the thousand years. The "abyss" (ἄβυσσον) is a prison for evil spirits (Rev. 20:7), and the New Testament indicates that when evil spirits are confined in this prison, they are prevented from participating in their normal demonic activities on earth (Luke 8:31; Rev. 9:1–3). For this reason, Satan can either be locked away in the abyss or he can be engaging in the various activities ascribed to him in the present age, but he cannot be both. The description of Satan's imprisonment in Revelation 20 is incompatible with the New Testament's portrayal of his influence during the church age, and therefore the binding of Satan cannot be understood as a present reality.[31]

---

[31] Waymeyer, *Amillennialism and the Age to Come,* 178. As Townsend summarizes: "During the millennium (Rev. 20) Satan will be completely cut off from the earth but during the present age he is vigorously active on the earth. Therefore the millennium cannot be the present age" (Jeffrey L.

Thus, this same will also be true for Satan when he is imprisoned in the abyss for one thousand years:

> The primary reason that Satan's imprisonment cannot be considered a present reality is because Revelation 20:1–3 is incompatible with the New Testament's portrayal of his influence during the present age. According to this passage, Satan will be cut off from all earthly activity during the thousand-year reign of Christ. The imagery of Satan being bound with a great chain and cast into the abyss—which is then shut and sealed over him—provides a vivid picture of the total removal of his influence on earth. In fact, if a vision were intended to teach that Satan is rendered completely inactive during the thousand years, it is difficult to imagine how this could have been portrayed more clearly.[32]

Vlach adds:

> Much attention often is given to whether the activities of Satan are curtailed or ceased, but before one even considers the activities of Satan, one must recognize what is happening to Satan himself, as a personal being. Satan himself is incarcerated and confined in a real place, a place called "the abyss." *Our point here is that not just a specific function of Satan (i.e., deceiving the nations) is hindered; Satan himself is absolutely confined to a place that results in a complete cessation of all that he does.*[33]

When Satan is imprisoned in the abyss, for the first time since Genesis 3, the whole world will no longer "lie in the power of the evil one" (1 John 5:19). Further, during Satan's one-thousand-year imprisonment, no longer will Satan have the power—nor the access—to blind the minds of the unbelieving, that they might not see the light of the Gospel of the Glory of Christ (2 Cor. 4:4)—who will be reigning on earth during that time. As Waymeyer summarizes:

> In contrast, the New Testament makes it abundantly clear that Satan . . . is extremely active on earth during the present age . . . It is impossible to

---

Townsend, "Is the Present Age the Millennium?," *BSac* 140, no. 559 [July 1983]: 216).

[32] Waymeyer, *Amillennialism and the Age to Come*, 177.

[33] Vlach, "The Kingdom of God and the Millennium," 246 (emphasis in the original).

reconcile this portrayal of Satan's activities in the present age with the view that he is currently sealed in the abyss.[34]

One final connective thought with what we have already seen: First Peter 3:19, as we saw earlier, is one of the places in the Bible that refers to the abyss as a prison: "in which also He went and made proclamation to the spirits now in *prison*." God does so again, as Revelation 20:3 shows: "and threw him into the abyss, and shut it and sealed it over him, so that he should not deceive the nations any longer, until the thousand years were completed; after these things he must be released for a short time." Revelation 20:7 tells of Satan's release from the abyss, only this time describes it by using the exact word that God's Word did in the 1 Peter 3:19 passage, but by not calling the place where Satan will be bound the abyss: "And when the thousand years are completed, Satan will be released from his *prison*." As before, so is true again: what is true for the abyss for the other demons when they are thrown into the prison of the abyss is true for Satan and the abyss, which will indeed be his prison for 1,000 years. The only way a demon can enter into or depart out of the prison of God's abyss—including Satan—is if the Godhead has a reason to let them out. Other than that, they do not go into the abyss by themselves, and they most certainly do not leave it by their strength or initiative.

New Testament Premillennial, Biblical, Doctrinal Truth #5: *Satan must be released for a short while after the thousand-year Millennial Kingdom (Rev. 20:7–10), in order for the Trinity to minutely fulfill Their faithfulness for all Their covenant promises and any other remaining promises and prophecies in Scripture, before the arrival of the new heavens and earth—and New Jerusalem.*

Though time did not permit further examination of the subject, both in the Faculty Lecture Series on "Premillennialism," nor in this journal article, this fifth New Testament premillennial biblical truth is also an incredibly important biblical doctrine. The journal article cited deals with its biblical explanation and significance in much more detail and should

---

[34] Waymeyer, *Amillennialism and the Age to Come*, 178.

be investigated for those who desire to follow this important biblical trail.[35]

SUMMARY AND SIGNIFICANCE

Although many people base their millennial views exclusively on or beginning with Revelation 20, we began elsewhere and limited ourselves to five essential premillennial truths from the New Testament. First, the real Triumphal Entry has not yet occurred (Matt. 21:1–11), because very specific promises and prophecies from the Davidic and Abrahamic Covenants—that must come true—await their fulfillment at Jesus' return. In Matthew 25:1–5, Jesus fulfilled with precision Zechariah 9:9, and was presented to Israel as her King. Yet Jesus did not fulfill in any way the next part—Zechariah 9:10—which contains two Davidic Covenant components, as well as establishes the Euphrates River as the northern boundary of the Abrahamic land promises. These Scriptures *must* be fulfilled at Jesus' next entry into Jerusalem and during His reign on earth.

Second, Christ Jesus did not accept the praise of the collective Jewish people at what most people call "the Triumphal Entry" (Matt. 21:1–11), but He vows to accept these exact praises—and many more—at some undisclosed time in the future from the descendants of these same Jewish people (Matt. 23:37–39), thus making Jesus' next entry into Jerusalem His real Triumphal Entry at the beginning of His Millennial Kingdom reign. In Matthew 21:8–11 the crowd shouted/sang Psalm 118:25–26 to Jesus, but He did not accept it from them at that time. We know this because later, at some of the last (if not the last) words of Jesus to the Jewish people before the events of the crucifixion were to begin, in Matthew 23:37–39, Jesus told the collective Jewish people (1) that their house was being left to them desolate—but not desolate forever, (2) that the collective Jewish people would not see Him again *until* they said, "Blessed is He who comes in the name of the LORD," using the same Psalm 118:26 that the masses had previously used a few days earlier, and

---

[35] Gregory H. Harris, "Must Satan Be Released? Indeed He Must Be: Toward a Biblical Understanding of Revelation 20:3," *The Master's Seminary Journal* 25/1 (Spring 2014): 11–27.

(3) that the requirement was mandatory that a remnant of those Jewish people's descendants must be maintained by God so that some subset of the Jewish people will fulfill the messianic Psalm 118:26 prophecy in reference to Jesus at His return. After all, paraphrasing Ezekiel 20:33: "As I live, I shall be King over you"—not just their Savior.

Third, Scripture repeatedly presents a God who will maintain and save a remnant of the Jewish people, beginning in the Tribulation and leading into the Millennial reign of Jesus. We were not able to cover this truth in detail, but a source was given for following the biblical trail that gives much biblical support for this premillennial doctrine. But even if we had only Matthew 21:1–11 and 23:37–39, these verses alone would *require* God to maintain the Jewish people, so that He can save a remnant of them at some undisclosed time in the future, who will indeed say to Him in praise and prophetic fulfillment: "Blessed is He who comes in the name of the LORD" (Ps. 118:26)—and Jesus will this time receive such praise due to Him, from these saved Jewish people.

Fourth: Satan is not currently bound in the abyss but will be bound there when Jesus Christ returns to earth to reign in the thousand-year Millennial Kingdom (Rev. 20:1–3), at whose conclusion Satan "must be released from the abyss for a short while." This is no small matter as to whether or not Satan is presently bound in the abyss or if that event awaits the return of Jesus. Biblical passages give a very descriptive list of the characteristics of the abyss and its inhabitants, such as Luke 8:28, Matthew 8:29; 1 Peter 3:19–20; 2 Peter 2:4, and Jude 6, and none of these verses show Satan sending forth demons or using the abyss for his own purposes (contra Storms, *Kingdom Come*), and these verses always present the abyss as a real and actual place of torment for demons over which God alone is the master. Not only is Satan not presently in the abyss, but the Bible definitively presents him with many current titles/attributes/activities that will no longer apply to him once Christ Jesus reigns on earth. Other than Satan's existence once he is confined in the abyss for a thousand years, *all* of the other titles/attributes/activities will be stripped from him—never to be returned, except for one completely limited exception, where Satan is allowed to function only to a degree as he has functioned before, in his temporary release from the abyss and his final rebellion, before being cast into eternal hell (Rev. 20:7–10).

In Revelation 20:1–3 (or elsewhere) Satan, although immensely powerful at this present time (Jude 6), is never referred to as the "king of the Abyss." As was true for hell and Hades, the abyss is for God's use alone—and never for Satan's. When Satan is captured as part of "the host on high" and thrown into the abyss in Revelation 20, he will be imprisoned in torment, at the very least, and he will suffer worse torment than other demons because of the unparalleled magnitude of his own sin; no one in all eternity has ever sinned against more light than Satan has. We also marked that Satan—in his basest form—is nonetheless only a demon. So when Satan and the remainder of the other demons, who comprise the evil part of the heavenly host, will be cast into the torment of the abyss, they will remain there until after many days, when they will be judged (Isa. 24:21–22). This initial confinement and torment will not be their final judgment nor their final destination; eventually all the demons who are in the abyss will be thrown into hell/the lake of fire, as disclosed in Revelation 20.

Fifth, while not able to develop this part in this article, Satan must be released for a short while after the thousand-year millennial kingdom (Rev. 20:7–10) in order for the Trinity to minutely fulfill their utter faithfulness for all of their covenant promises and any other remaining promises and prophecies in Scripture, thus summing up all things in Christ, which the Godhead has been doing so faithfully from Genesis 1 onward into the ushering in of the eternal state in Revelation 21–22.

FULL BIBLIOGRAPHIC INFORMATION

Chapter One—Gregory H. Harris, "Satan's Work as a Deceiver," *Bibliotheca Sacra*. 156:2 (Apr–June 1999), 190–202. Used by permission.

Chapter Two—Gregory H. Harris, "Satan's Deceptive Miracles in the Tribulation," *Bibliotheca Sacra*. 156:3 (July–Sept 1999), 308–24. Used by permission.

Chapter Three— Gregory H. Harris "Does God Deceive? Towards a Biblical Understanding of the 'Deluding Influence' of 2 Thessalonians 2:11," *The Master's Seminary Journal* 16:1 (Spring 2005), 73–93. Used by permission.

Chapter Four—Gregory H. Harris, "The Wound of the Beast in the Tribulation," *Bibliotheca Sacra*. 156:4 (Oct–Dec 1999), 459–68. Used by permission.

Chapter Five—Gregory H. Harris, "Can Satan Raise the Dead? Toward a Biblical View of the Beast's Wound," *The Master's Seminary Journal* 18:1 (Spring 2007), 23–41. Used by permission.

Chapter Six—Gregory H. Harris, "Premillennialism in the New Testament: Five Biblically Doctrinal Truths," *The Master's Seminary Journal* 29:2 (Fall 2018), 177–205. Used by permission.

www.ingramcontent.com/pod-product-compliance
Lightning Source LLC
Chambersburg PA
CBHW011319080526
44589CB00018B/2731